EDUCATING THE HEART AND MIND

A History of Marymount School

1926-2001

By Joanne Safian, RSHM

Published by Marymount School
1026 Fifth Avenue
New York, New York 10028
Printed in the U.S.A.
For all general information contact Marymount School at:
Telephone 212 744-4486
Fax 212 744-0163
E mail history@marymount.k12.ny.us
Visit us on the Internet at http://www.marymount.k12.ny.us

Reprinted articles on pages 17 and 18 are used with permission
of The New York Times

Printed in Italy by Graphicom, Verona

*This publication was made possible
through the generous support of the
Marymount Alumnae and Parents' Associations.*

*This history is dedicated to
the Religious of the Sacred Heart of Mary
and the faculty and staff, past and present,
who have devoted their knowledge and
talents to the students of Marymount School.*

*"The aims of a Marymount
education are manifold:
to educate the heart and mind,
and to provide for
each student's total growth,
intellectually, spiritually,
socially, and physically."*

Mother Marie Joseph Butler, RSHM

CONTENTS

ROM THE Roaring Twenties to the New Millennium; from an initial enrollment of thirteen students to a current enrollment of approximately 500 students in Nursery through Class XII; from one building on the corner of 84th Street and Fifth Avenue to four buildings, one of them the new home of the Middle School on 82nd Street just off Fifth Avenue; from a foundation established by the Religious of the Sacred Heart of Mary to an independent school governed by a Board of Trustees and a lay and religious staff of 120:

For 75 years, the doors of Marymount School have opened to welcome students, faculty and staff, parents, and alumnae into historic school buildings and into a remarkable educational experience. Over the 75 years, Marymount's enrollment, facilities, and organizational structure have grown and changed. At the same time, the focus on excellence, emphasis on religious values and the commitment to the education of women have never wavered. The school's founder, Mother Marie Joseph Butler, RSHM, stated, "The aims of a Marymount education are manifold: to educate the heart and mind, and to provide for each student's total growth, intellectually, spiritually, socially, and physically." The Goals and Criteria established in 1991 by the international network of Marymount Schools echo the same values—a life-long love of learning, a relationship with God, a sense of social justice, an appreciation of diversity, and an affirmation of personal growth. Marymount's own Strategic Plan, approved by the Board of Trustees on June 3, 1998, articulates a similar sense of purpose: "With an inclusive school community and a rigorous and values-centered educational program, the School will challenge its students intellectually, encourage reflection and spiritual growth, and offer opportunities to practice moral and ethical choice. Marymount will continue to develop confident, knowledgeable and competent young women who are able to contribute to and influence their environment and their world in the next century."

What follows is the story of Marymount's growth in realizing the founder's vision for each new generation.

INTRODUCTION

A view of Béziers, in the south-central part of France

HE INSTITUTE of the Religious of the Sacred Heart of Mary was founded in Béziers, France, in 1849, when a young widow, Appollonie (Mère St. Jean) Pelissier-Cure, in collaboration with a parish priest, Père Jean Antoine Gailhac, inspired a group of women to come together, dedicating themselves to serve God and minister to the needs and education of young women. From that beginning, the Religious of the Sacred Heart of Mary grew into an international congregation in 14 countries on four continents. Today, the ministries of the Religious of the Sacred Heart of Mary have become more varied in response to the needs of the Church and the times, but the order's Mission Statement affirms a unified purpose: "As we become more deeply inserted in the realities of the Church and the world, we use our individual and corporate talents to work creatively in diverse ministries for the promotion of justice." Marymount School's goal, as stated in its own Mission Statement, to "educate young women who continue to question, risk, and grow. . . care, serve, and lead . . . and are prepared to challenge, shape, and change the world" is fully consonant with the mission of the Religious of the Sacred Heart of Mary throughout the world.

As the Religious of the Sacred Heart of Mary grew, they were invited by bishops in various countries to begin educational ministries in Portugal, Ireland, England and, eventually, the United States. The first group of RSHM came to the United States in 1877 to Sag Harbor, at the end of Long Island, in New York, the present location of Cormaria, a retreat center.

In 1903, Mother Marie Joseph Butler, who had entered the religious community in Béziers, and spent years subsequently in Portugal, came to the United States and began her ministry at St. Mary's Parish School in Long Island City. In 1907, Mother Butler, with other Religious of the Sacred Heart of Mary, opened the first Marymount on the Reynard Estate in Tarrytown, which had been located for the religious

Chapter One:
THE HERITAGE

Reynard Estate, Tarrytown, New York. Site of the first Marymount

Marymount, Neuilly, France. Established 1923

Marymount, Los Angeles. Established 1923

Marymount, Rome. Established 1930

community by Mother Butler's cousin James, in honor of his deceased wife. James Butler, a benefactor of more than one Marymount, emigrated to the United States from Ireland in 1875 and eventually made his fortune in the grocery business. Today, the site is the home of Marymount Convent (the province retirement center), several small communities of RSHM, the provincial offices of the Eastern American Province of the Religious of the Sacred Heart of Mary

and Marymount College (soon to be known as Marymount College of Fordham University). In 1923, Mother Butler founded Marymount in Neuilly, a suburb of Paris, the first international school established by a United States educational organization.

The same year marked the founding of Marymount in Los Angeles, and in subsequent years, other Marymount schools and colleges were founded in the United States and abroad.

1848
Meeting in Seneca Falls, New York, calls for equal rights for American women

1861-65
U.S. Civil War

1876
Alexander Graham Bell invents the telephone

James Butler is seen here with his grandchildren, several of whom were among the first students at Marymount School when it opened in 1926.

JAMES BUTLER, Marymount's first benefactor, emigrated from Ireland to the United States in 1875 and eventually became a caterer for the Windsor Hotel in New York City. While there, he formed a partnership with another Irish immigrant to begin a chain of grocery stores. By the time James Butler was 29, he was able to buy out his partner and name his growing chain James Butler, Incorporated. By 1909, his stores had annual sales of $15 million. In 1929, he owned 1,100 stores. A long time interest in horse racing led him to establish Yonkers Raceway.

Butler's financial success allowed him to be very generous to the Catholic church, but the primary object of his beneficence was always Marymount. He and his wife, Mary Ann, supported the vision of his cousin Mother Butler to found an institute of higher learning for young Catholic women. He helped fund the purchase of the Reynard Estate in Tarrytown, which became the first Marymount, and the Vanderbilt-Burden Mansion at 1028 Fifth Avenue, which became Marymount School of New York.

Butler held in high esteem the education offered by the Religious of the Sacred Heart of Mary. Ten of his grandchildren attended Marymount Fifth Avenue, several of them among the first 13 students to enter the school in February 1926.

Mr. Butler died in 1934 after a long illness and was buried with his wife and son in the crypt under the chapel at Marymount in Tarrytown.

1877
Thomas A. Edison invents the record player

1908
Henry Ford produces the first Model T car

1914-1918
World War I

RSHM Founders: Père Jean Antoine Gailhac and Mère St. Jean Pelissier-Cure

THE RELIGIOUS OF THE SACRED HEART OF MARY, an international apostolic institute of religious women, was founded on February 24, 1849, in Béziers, an ancient hilltop city in the south of France. For some time, Père Jean Antoine Gailhac, a priest who had been born in Béziers in 1802, had seen the need for a religious order dedicated to the work of the Good Shepherd Refuge (a shelter) and Orphanage which were under his care. Among those who shared his vision was Appollonie Pelissier-Cure, who was born in 1809 in Murveil, France, and married a lawyer named Eugène Cure. Cure was a lifelong friend of Gailhac's. The priest frequently visited with the Cures, and they gave financial support to their friend's ministry. In 1848, Eugène Cure died of a massive stroke.

Three months later, Appollonie decided to enter religious life and, in so doing, made Gailhac's dream of a religious order a reality. On February 24, 1849, Appollonie (Mère St. Jean) Cure, Eulalie (Mère Ste. Croix) Vidal, Rosalie (Mère St. Stanislas) Gibbal, Rose (Soeur St. Modeste) Jeantet, Cécile (Soeur St. Aphrodise) Cambon, and Marie (Soeur Ste. Agnes) Roques, assumed responsibility for the work of the Good Shepherd Refuge and Orphanage. These six women comprised the founding community of a new Institute, that of the Sacred Heart of Mary. Mère St. Jean Cure, considered the order's co-founder with Gailhac, became the first general superior.

The early years of the new religious order were marked by both challenge and growth. The task of running the Orphanage, and the Preservation (a ministry to rescue and educate girls who would otherwise find themselves on the street), as well as a boarding school, were formidable, and low funds caused by blights on the order's vineyards added to the difficulties. Nevertheless, by the time of Mère St. Jean's death on March 4, 1869, 72 women had joined the order, and initial efforts had been made to establish foundations in Ireland and England.

By 1874, the Institute numbered 140, with foundations in Ireland (1870), Portugal (1871), and England (1872). The first foundation in the United States was established on Long Island in Sag Harbor, New York, in 1877, several years before Père Gailhac's death at the age of 88 on January 25, 1890.

Both Père Gailhac and Mère St. Jean Cure are buried in the crypt beneath the chapel of the Motherhouse in Béziers.

Today, the Religious of the Sacred Heart of Mary are 1,100 in number. They are established in fourteen countries on four continents and carry out their mission "to know and celebrate God's love for us and to make that love known to others."

*Père Jean
Antoine Gailhac*

*Mère Saint Jean
Pelissier-Cure*

Mother Marie Joseph Butler, RSHM (1860-1940)

BORN JOHANNA BUTLER ON JULY 22, 1860, at The Rower in County Kilkenny, Ireland, the seventh child of Ellen and John Butler, Mother Marie Joseph Butler was the founder of Marymount School. At the age of sixteen, she chose to enter religious life and became a novice of the Religious of the Sacred Heart of Mary in Béziers, France. While still a novice, she was sent to Portugal, where she took her vows in 1880 and proved herself an able student of the Portuguese language and an effective teacher. Despite the government's hostility toward religious groups, Mother Butler was instrumental, as both a religious superior and an educational leader, in preserving and expanding the order's schools during her eighteen years in Portugal.

In 1903, Mother Butler was sent to the United States and entrusted with the expansion of the Religious of the Sacred Heart of Mary's work in this country. At St. Mary's Parish School in Long Island City, Mother Butler ensured that the nuns earned their teaching certification and that the new school expanded its enrollment and curriculum. In the next several years, Mother Butler oversaw the establishment of parish schools in other areas of New York City, including Brooklyn and the Bronx.

However, it was Mother Butler's interest in higher education for women that led to the founding of the first Marymount. Assisted by her cousin James Butler, who wished to honor the memory of his deceased wife, Mother Butler acquired property for a school and college in Tarrytown, New York, in 1906. In this new endeavor, she was assisted by Mother Gerard Phelan, who had served as headmistress of the Sacred Heart of Mary Convent School in Seafield, Liverpool, England, and who would become Mother Butler's educational collaborator. The school formally opened in 1907. In 1910, a novitiate was established, and in 1918, adjacent property was acquired to allow the college division to expand into a four-year degree-granting institution, confirming the RSHM commitment to higher education for women. Mother Butler was listed as president of the college and Mother Gerard Phelan as dean.

Mother Butler's interest in the education of young women was not only visionary during this era when women won the right to vote, but geographically far-reaching as well. In 1923, she established schools in Los Angeles, in Neuilly, a suburb of Paris, and Marymount School, New York City in 1926. She also established the first study-abroad program in the United States at Marymount College in Tarrytown.

Mother Marie Joseph Butler

Months after the founding of Marymount in New York City, Mother Butler was elected the fifth General Superior of the Religious of the Sacred Heart of Mary and thus assumed stewardship for the entire congregation and its works. During her tenure, foundations and schools of the Religious of the Sacred Heart of Mary were established in Brazil (1927) and Italy (1930), and were extended throughout France, Portugal, Great Britain, Ireland, and the United States, constituting an international network that remains to this day.

Mother Butler served as General Superior of the order for fourteen years, until her death at Tarrytown in 1940. She is buried in the crypt beneath the Butler Memorial Chapel at the Marymount Convent in Tarrytown. Her cousins, Mother Gerard Phelan and James Butler, are buried beside her.

Junior School students, c. 1928

B Y 1926, the year Marymount School was founded, the RSHM's reputation for educating women was well established. Mother Butler's vision, formed before women won the right to vote, included strong conviction regarding the role of women and the importance of their education. Her words continue to resonate today, "The world never needed women's intelligence and sympathy more than it does today."

The school was founded in response to requests from Marymount, Tarrytown, alumnae who sought a day school for their children in New York City. Assisted by her cousin Beatrice Butler (Mrs. Philip MacGuire), daughter of James Butler, Mother Butler succeeded in finding the Fifth Avenue location. James Butler helped finance the purchase. The contract was signed on December 31, 1925, and 1028 Fifth Avenue became Marymount School.

Although the 1028 building is known as the Vanderbilt-Burden mansion, its first owners were Jonathan and Harriet Thorne. Jonathan Thorne, the son of a successful merchant, made his own fortune in the leather business. The 1028 building was his retirement house. Interestingly, the *Annals*, written by Mother du Carmel Connolly, record that in 1965, both Victoria and Harriet Weaver, great-granddaughter and granddaughter of the original owners, visited Marymount on separate occasions. Mrs. Weaver had lived in 1028 until she was eleven years old. When Jonathan Thorne died in 1920, the house was sold to Florence Vanderbilt Burden, the granddaughter of William Henry Vanderbilt and the great-granddaughter of Cornelius Vanderbilt.

When Marymount was purchased, the neighborhood was changing from rows of single-family dwellings to luxury apartment buildings that were easier to manage and staff but were still spacious and elegant. Nevertheless, the neighborhood would still be recognizable today. The Metropolitan Museum of Art

Chapter Two:
MARYMOUNT SCHOOL
FOUNDATION AND
EARLY YEARS

Founder's Day celebration, 1927

was not as large, but it did extend as far north. Central Park did not have its transverse road at 84th Street, but carriages did travel through the park.

Stories surrounding the founding of the school testify to beginnings rooted in both faith and determined hard work.

An oft-repeated story, recorded in Katherine Burton's *Mother Butler of Marymount* and reputed to have been related to Mother Butler by Father John O'Rourke S.J. of the nearby Church of St. Ignatius Loyola, concerns a 1911 "prophecy" about Marymount. In that year, Father O'Rourke received a call to attend to a dying person in residence at 1028. This person was a daughter of the Kinsella family, servants who were caring for the house while the family was away for the summer. Just before the little girl died, she told her mother that someday nuns would live in the house. The girl's mother thought this was a very odd thing for her daughter to say, but she related it to Father O'Rourke anyway. The 1915 census records do

MARYMOUNT SCHOOL

1028 FIFTH AVENUE, NEW YORK CITY

DEDICATION CEREMONIES

BLESSING OF BUILDING   - - -   Rt. Rev. John J. Dunn, D. D.

HOLY MASS   - - - - - -   Rt. Rev. John J. Dunn, D. D.

Petit déjeuner in Assembly Hall
Reception to His Lordship Bishop Dunn in Reception Room

OVERTURE   - - - - - - -   Miss E. Dawson

ADDRESS OF WELCOME - - - -   Miss Marion Hanrehan

AVE MARIA—GOUNOD   - - -   Miss Virginia Brodel

PIANO SOLO - - - - - - -   Mrs. E. P. Bahutge

VOCAL SELECTIONS - - - - -   Countess K. de Prorok

LAST ROSE OF SUMMER   - - -   Miss A. Robinson

ADDRESS   - - - - - - -   Hon. Victor J. Dowling

EPISCOPAL BLESSING - - - -   Rt. Rev. John J. Dunn, D. D.

The Dedication Ceremonies program,
February 2, 1926

1920

19th Amendment
passes, giving women
the right to vote   *Prohibition begins*

1921
Warren Harding
becomes President

BURDEN HOME TO BE A SCHOOL FOR GIRLS

Residence at 5th Av. and 84th St. Bought by Order of the Sacred Heart of Mary.

A GIFT OF JAMES BUTLER

Students to Get Religious Training as Safeguard Against "Social-ism and Chaos."

The former residence of Mrs. Florence Vanderbilt Burden, on the south corner of Eighty-fourth Street and Fifth Avenue, has been purchased by the Order of the Sacred Heart of Mary and will be used as a select school for girls in connection with Marymount College at Tarrytown-on-Hudson.

Mrs. Burden is a daughter of Mrs. Hamilton McK. Twombly, who a few days ago sold her home on the south-west corner of Fifty-fourth Street and Fifth Avenue to John D. Rockefeller Jr. for a figure said to have been considerably in excess of $1,000,000.

James Butler the Donor.

The purchase of the Burden house by the Order of the Sacred Heart of Mary

was made possible by a gift of James Butler, the donor of the original Marymount School and College at Tarrytown-on-Hudson. The house just purchased is 1,028 Fifth Avenue and is a five-and-a-half-story white stone structure in the French Renaissance style of architecture. It stands on a lot fronting 25 feet on the avenue and having a depth of 100 feet. It was built in 1912 from plans by C. P. H. Gilbert and is assessed by the City of New York for taxation purposes at about $400,000, of which $220,000 represents land value.

The property was chosen by Mrs. Philip D. MacGuire, a daughter of James Butler, because of its location and adaptability to the needs of a school for girls. According to Mrs. MacGuire few alterations will be necessary, as the rooms are large, well ventilated and capable of accommodating about 100 pupils.

To Be Dedicated Feb. 2.

The new Marymount School will be dedicated and blessed on Feb. 2, Feast of the Purification of Our Lady, by Bishop Dunn, who also will sing the mass. The alumnae and friends of Marymount, Tarrytown, will be invited to assist at the ceremonies. Enrolment of pupils will take place on Monday, Feb. 1, at 9 o'clock.

"The purpose of establishing a school in the city," Mrs. MacGuire said, "is to give the same scientific, cultural and religious training which have contributed to the unique success of Marymount School and to afford an opportunity to those who could not be accommodated there to experience the value of a genuine religious training, which educators like Dr. Butler, the President of Columbia, are beginning to realize is essential as the only safeguard against socialism and chaos."

Brown, Wheelock; Harris, Vought & Co. negotiated the sale of the property.

corroborate the presence of a Kinsella family in the house. Margaret Kinsella was the housekeeper and Thomas Kinsella was termed a "driver." However intriguing the "prophecy," it was hard work that enabled Marymount to open its doors in a month. The school *Annals* record that when the religious arrived at 1028 just after New Year's Day, "the condition of the walls and ceilings in every room from basement to roof left much to be desired. Days (and sometimes nights) of constant labor and fatigue were endured. As a change from the routine drudgery of cleaning walls, floors, etc., Mother Butler had her group of workers arranging and hanging art work such as a Madonna Del Gran Duca painting in the foyer. . . ." Another account tells us that workmen were still laying carpet on February 1, 1926, the day classes

Article from The New York Times, *December 31, 1925 ("1912" date cited in article should be 1902)*

The Dedication Mass on February 2, 1926 in the school's first chapel on the second floor of 1028. Mother Butler is pictured to the right of Bishop John Dunn and to the left is Mother Gerard Phelan. Students from Marymount College in Tarrytown also attended in their academic robes. Mother Butler's handwriting at the bottom of the picture identifies the individuals.

1921	1922	1924
Edith Warton wins Pulitzer Prize for Age of Innocence	*Willa Cather wins Pulitzer Prize for* One of Ours	*Calvin Coolidge becomes 30th President*

began. Rather than risk their leaving and not finishing, Mother Butler had supper served to them. They finished their work at 11:00 p.m. Mother Butler's determination and farsightedness is also evident in her decision, during the coal strike of January 1926, to change to oil, a new way of heating at the time.

Besides Mother Butler, the Religious assigned to the preparation of the house and the opening of the school included Mother Baptiste Holohan, Mother Stanislaus Clarke; two novices, M. Albert Higgins and M. Catherine Garvey; a postulant, Sister Walburga Gaffney; and Sisters Alexandria, Anthony Lynch, Martha Mythen, Winifred Russell, and Columba Dougherty. One suspects that without the efforts of these remarkable women, some of whom later served as founding sisters or superiors in other RSHM ministries,

the school could never have been ready in little more than a month after the building was purchased.

The school officially opened on the Feast of the Purification, February 2, 1926, with a dedication ceremony and liturgy conducted by Most Reverend John J. Dunn, Bishop of New York, and an address given by Justice Victor Dowling that paid tribute to both Mother Butler and James Butler. Several students from Marymount College in Tarrytown, as well as other invited guests, were also present.

For the first six months, the local religious community in residence consisted of Mother Ignatius Kearney, who assumed the major responsibility for the school and served as Mother Superior, Mother Genevieve Toner, Sister Anthony Lynch, and Sister Martha Mythen. In September, Mother Elizabeth

MARYMOUNT SCHOOL IN 5TH AV. DEDICATED

Right Rev. J. J. Dunn Presides at Exercises—Justice V. J. Dowling Is a Speaker.

The dedication ceremonies of the new Marymount School, recently opened in the former residence of Mrs. Florence Vanderbilt Burden on the southeast corner of Fifth Avenue and Eighty-fourth Street, took place yesterday morning. The Right Rev. John J. Dunn, Auxiliary Bishop of New York, officiated and celebrated mass in the school chapel preceding the ceremony.

The new school is under the direction of the Religious of the Sacred Heart of Mary, whose mother house is in France, and the Vicariate at Marymount College, Tarrytown-on-the-Hudson. The building was purchased by the Order of the Sacred Heart of Mary following a gift made by James Butler, donor of the original Marymount School and College at Tarrytown.

Members of the Marymount Alumnae Association received the guests. Miss Marion Hanrehan, President of the alumnae, made an address of welcome. Among the singers on the musical program was the Countess Byron Khun de Prorok, an alumna of Marymount College, formerly Miss Alice J. Kenny, daughter of Mr. and Mrs. William Francis Kenny of 820 Fifth Avenue. Justice Victor J. Dowling of the Appellate Division paid a tribute to James Butler, as did Bishop Dunn.

A New York Times article, February 3, 1926, noting the school's February 2nd dedication

Through this entrance came the first students of Marymount.

The entrance to 1028 Fifth Avenue, located on 84th Street

1924	1925	1927
E.M. Forster's A Passage to India is published	*F. Scott Fitzgerald's The Great Gatsby is published*	*Charles Lindberg makes the first nonstop solo transatlantic flight*

Gallagher and Sister Angela Martin joined the original group, thus creating a community of six Religious. Mother Butler became General Superior of the Religious of the Sacred Heart of Mary in April 1926, but despite her responsibilities for an international congregation, the large number of American foundations allowed her to spend much time in the United States. Visits to Marymount Fifth Avenue were frequent, especially on feast days.

The religious were assisted by a group of lay teachers. Among those whose names recur in the early records are Helen Dwyer, Marion Hanrahan, Norah Smaridge, Sis Driscoll, Anne Robinson, Frances Baker, Anne Rogan, and Hazel McGuckin.

Classes began with thirteen students. Lou Ellen Creamer '36 remembered being the first student to walk through the doors on the day the school opened. She recalled wearing a navy blue uniform with a white collar and having a more formal uniform for special events, such as for Mother Butler's visits. She recalled Norah Smaridge as being a marvelous teacher of English, and she remembered Mother Elizabeth Gallagher and Mother Genevieve Toner, both of whom returned to work at Marymount in later years.

In succeeding years, the school continued to grow, and its traditions developed. Trips to The Metropolitan Museum of Art across the street began immediately. In the 1926-27 school year, the Dramatic Club was established, and a year later, the first yearbook, the *Marifia*, was published. The name is a contraction of "Marymount Fifth Avenue," as the school was often fondly called, distinguishing it from other schools in the Marymount network. It was also in that year that Halloween parties seem to have begun and a Christmas play was performed. Members of the sodality (a religious and service organization) were first received into the Children of Mary, and on May 5th,

Parlor floor

Library, c. 1929

First chapel. In the 1930s, the chapel was moved to the front room of the Parlor floor in 1028. In the 1950s, when the 1026 building was purchased, the chapel was enlarged and reached across the front of the 1026 and 1027 Parlor floors.

1928
Margaret Mead publishes Coming of Age in Samoa

1927
Holland Tunnel opens

1929
Stock market crashes on October 29

fourteen children received their First Communion. In June 1928, the school graduated its first class, consisting of two seniors: Elizabeth Byrne and Marjorie McCormack. Enrollment grew, and by the 1928-29 school year, 68 students were enrolled.

Meanwhile, the building itself continued to require work; partitions were removed to create larger classrooms, and more radiators were installed. With the building now considered a school rather than a private dwelling, additional changes were needed to satisfy fire codes, and insurance provisions, and to acquire a certificate of occupancy.

Elizabeth Byrne and Marjorie McCormack
First graduates, 1928

A Junior School classroom, 1928

Junior School Christmas celebration c.1920

The first Marifia, *1928*

Junior School students celebrating Mother Joseph Butler's feast day

A drama presentation celebrating George Washington's birthday, 1928

The world never needed women's intelligence and sympathy more than it does today. The education that will equip women to meet modern conditions effectively will not neglect any medium in which true American womanhood may find its best expression.

Mother Marie Joseph Butler, RSHM
FOUNDER OF MARYMOUNT SCHOOL

The Marymount School Buildings

1028 Fifth Avenue

I N 1925, Mother Butler purchased 1028 Fifth Avenue to become the home of Marymount School. The house was built in 1901-1903 for Jonathan Thorne, a leather merchant, who hired the mansion specialist C.P.H. Gilbert. The architect developed a limestone *beaux arts* style facade, with the main entrance through a swell-front and a pair of Ionic columns, but set off from the street by a deep basement behind a handsome balustrade. Gilbert, who also designed the Jewish Museum building at 92nd Street and Fifth Avenue and the Ukrainian Institute at 79th Street, repeated the double-column theme in the stairhall. The townhouses at 1026 and 1027 Fifth Avenue were designed by the architectural firm of Van Vleck and Goldsmith and were built on speculation in 1901-03 for Benjamin Williams.

In 1936, as Marymount expanded and as the rich moved to apartment buildings, the school bought the adjacent 1027 Fifth Avenue, forty feet wide and the most expensive house built for sale in New York when it was erected. Benjamin Williams had his architects finish the house "on a magnificent scale," according to *The New York Times* of 1906. He sold it to George Crawford Clark, a banker, who paid $540,000. Later alterations make it difficult to determine what elements survive from the original construction, but they must include the lavish marble-and-tile entryway and marble wainscotting in the main hall. The milk-white marble facade made the house unusual, even on a Fifth Avenue of millionaires.

In 1919, Herbert Lee Pratt bought 1027 Fifth Avenue, and he redecorated several rooms, one of which was the front room on the second floor. Pratt had that room panelled after the eighteenth century drawing room of Wingerworth Manor, in Derbyshire, and it held Mr. Pratt's collection of American portraits.

In 1950, Marymount bought Williams' other building, 1026 Fifth Avenue. First occupied by Mary Kingsland, a banker's widow, it was sold to Dunlevy Milbank, one of New York's leading philanthropists, after Mrs. Kingsland's death in 1919. In slight contrast to its mate,1026 has a limestone facade. Noteworthy inside is the panelled, Tudor-style reception room at the rear, one of Marymount's finest interiors, along with its magnificently tiled bathroom.

Marymount's newest building, the Albert Gould Jennings house at 2 East 82nd Street, was built in 1900 for Jennings, an investor and society figure, a prominent amateur golfer and a charter member of the Tuxedo Club, in Tuxedo, New York. Jennings owned the house until 1938. The *beaux arts* style front, with its pleasing contrast of deep-red brick and soft white marble, was designed by Schickel & Ditmars. Coincidentally, those architects designed many buildings familiar to the Marymount community, including the Church of St. Ignatius Loyola on 84th Street and Park Avenue (1900), the Dominican Fathers Priory at 65th Street and Lexington Avenue (1881), and St. Joseph's Church on 87th Street near First Avenue (1895).

Construction of The Metropolitan Museum of Art's "North Wing," showing Marymount's three buildings across Fifth Avenue, c. 1907

A benign conversion to apartments in 1939 assured that Marymount acquired this building almost perfectly intact with speaking tubes, marble fireplaces, old pushbutton electric switches, and stained glass and delicate plaster ornamentation like that in the music room, with images of flutes and violins worked into the detail. The panelled library on the fourth floor is particularly fine. These architectural details are familiar to the Marymount community from the first three buildings. It is astonishing that such work has survived.

Marymount's new Middle School building received this enviable review in the Architectural Annual in 1901: "It addresses the beholder frankly, a finished design tempered with exquisite restraint. Every detail has been treated with judgment and good taste." A compliment (and a challenge) for Marymount in the twenty-first century!

By CHRISTOPHER GRAY, father of Olivia, '06
"Streetscapes" Columnist, Sunday Real Estate Section
The New York Times

2 East 82nd Street

These women were among the founding members of Marymount School and served in various leadership roles at the school throughout the years

Sister Ignatius Kearney, RSHM (1891-1979)
At Marymount School 1926-1932

Born in Ireland in 1891, Sister Ignatius entered religious life on December 8, 1910, as one of the first two RSHM postulants to receive her religious training in the United States. Sister Ignatius was the superior of the school's religious community at the time of the opening of Marymount School in 1926. She had previously taught at Marymount Academy in Tarrytown, and earned her Ph.D. in French from Fordham University. Sister Ignatius brought to Marymount both scholarship and experience. She guided the school through its early growth, the challenge of the 1929 stock market crash and the emergence of a junior college division at the Marymount Fifth Avenue school.

In 1932, Sister Ignatius left Marymount Fifth Avenue for subsequent assignments at RSHM schools in Los Angeles, California and Sag Harbor, New York, and at the college at Tarrytown. She was the author of *Foundations of Faith*, a history of the foundations of the Religious of the Sacred Heart of Mary in the United States. She died in Tarrytown on September 25, 1979.

Two former students and colleagues of Sister Ignatius remember her as a woman who inspired a love of learning and a sense of self-confidence in her students:

> In my last conversation with Sister Ignatius, she chided me because I had not yet read the full text of the Solzhenitsyn address given at Harvard a few weeks before. Two weeks later she sent it to me in the mail lest I neglect it once again. I recall this because it symbolized so much of all Sister Ignatius did for me. She gave me a great love of learning; better still, she taught me that this love could lead me to God. (SISTER COLETTE MAHONEY, RSHM, former president of Marymount Manhattan College)

And another tribute:

> I've often thought about how she drew us to accomplish what we did. She didn't seem to be trying to be 'relevant,' though her immersion both in the classics and in contemporary thought was evident. Quite simply, she just seemed to presume that we could do anything. She seemed to see us at our best and make us feel comfortable there.
>
> (SISTER JACQUELYN PORTER, RSHM, Professor of Theology at Marymount University, Arlington, Virginia)

This photo, found in the Marymount Los Angeles archives, shows Mother Butler, then General Superior of the RSHM (center), with Mother Gerard Phelan pictured to the left and Mother Ignatius Kearney to the right.

Sister Elizabeth Gallagher, RSHM
At Marymount School 1926-1940, 1941-1942, 1966-1992

Born in 1905 in Ireland, Sister Elizabeth Gallagher joined the Religious of the Sacred Heart of Mary in 1924. In September 1926, just a few months after professing her vows, she joined the faculty of Marymount School Fifth Avenue in its first full year of operation. She stayed at the school until 1940, spent a year at Marymount Los Angeles, and returned to Marymount Fifth Avenue for two more years.

For the next two decades, Sister Elizabeth was engaged in a variety of impressive educational endeavors: she taught at RSHM schools in Sag Harbor, New York and Quebec, Canada; in 1949, she went to Arlington, Virginia as superior of the religious community and subsequently served as the first president of Marymount Junior College.

In 1955, she founded the Marymount International School in Kingston, Surrey, England, and in 1961, she travelled to Marymount in Rome to build the boarding school at via di Villa Lauchli. After her worldwide travels, she returned to Marymount Fifth Avenue in 1966 as librarian and to work in the Business office

Sister Elizabeth retired in 1992 and was honored at the liturgical celebration of the 75th Anniversary of Marymount School on February 4, 2001 for her 75 years of involvement with the school.

Sister Genevieve Toner, RSHM (1900-1989)
At Marymount School 1926-1934, 1966-1984

A New York City native, Sister Genevieve was born in 1900 and entered the Religious of the Sacred Heart of Mary in Tarrytown in 1923. Sister Genevieve was at Marymount School Fifth Avenue from the beginning, a member of the first religious community in residence in February 1926. In the early years, she taught various classes in the Lower School, and American history and mathematics in the Upper School.

In 1934, Sister Genevieve left Marymount Fifth Avenue and did not return for thirty-two years. During that time, she earned a Master's degree in Library Science and was teacher and librarian at New York RSHM schools at Sag Harbor, Garden City, St. Thomas Aquinas School in the Bronx, and the Marymount International School in Rome.

In 1966, she returned to Marymount and managed library, bookkeeping, and various business office affairs until her retirement in 1984.

On November 7, 1989, Sister Genevieve Toner died at the Marymount Convent in Tarrytown.

Sister Marie du Carmel Connolly, RSHM (1899-2000)
At Marymount School 1927-1954, 1961-1968

Born on April 1, 1899, in Ireland, Sister du Carmel entered the Religious of the Sacred Heart of Mary in 1923, at Tarrytown, and was one of the pioneer RSHM to establish Marymount Fifth Avenue. Arriving at the school in 1927, Sister du Carmel filled many roles, including teacher, superior of the religious community, and Junior School divisional head. Like many of her fellow religious, she was a respected and innovative educator. Among the first to explore the curriculum that was known as the "New Math," Sister du Carmel helped revise the mathematics program in the Junior School. In the years that Sister du Carmel was not at Marymount School, she held positions as teacher or librarian in a variety of RSHM schools—in Tarrytown and Garden City, New York; Quebec, Canada; and St. Louis, Missouri.

On returning to Marymount School in 1961 to work in the library and the archives, Sister du Carmel began writing her history of the school, and it is for these *Annals* that she will be especially remembered. Filling two archival storage boxes, her story of the school from 1926 to 1961 extends for 236 pages, with additional annual supplements from 1962 to 1968.

Her *Annals* afford a vivid picture of daily life at the school, detailing the activities of students and faculty, including awards won, conferences attended, visitors welcomed, traditions carried on, and special events celebrated. Her work has served as a primary source during the writing of this 75th Anniversary history of the school.

When she retired to Marymount Convent at Tarrytown, she continued to be an educator and librarian, posting daily thought-provoking quotations that she selected from books or newspapers.

Sister du Carmel died on November 30, 2000, at the Marymount Convent in Tarrytown at the age of 101.

Junior School students in the 1027 lobby

T HE OCTOBER 1929 stock market crash and the advent of the Great Depression made its impact on both students and the school. In 1932, one in four Americans was unemployed, and in 1933, the value of stock on the New York Stock Exchange was less than a fifth of what it had been prior to the crash. Genevieve Travers '36 remembers her father coming home and going directly to bed, so upset was he at how badly many of his friends were faring. Other alumnae remember people selling apples on the street. Marymount students filled baskets with food, clothing, and toys for needy families.

School records of the time indicate that enrollment slowed during the early 1930s, not surprisingly during a period when 13 million Americans were unemployed. The school remained solvent, since Marymount's expenses never exceeded its income, but there was never much of a balance carried over to the next year. The worst year for Marymount was 1935-36, but the school had begun some serious belt tightening measures during the 1932-33 school year. The school was able to lower its mortgage payments to Marymount Tarrytown, and for a few years they may have paid only the interest on the loan. The sisters also spent less on groceries (primarily purchased from James Butler, Inc.), labor, repairs, equipment, and salaries. There were only two lay teachers in 1932, both of whom had been with the school from the beginning, but Marymount, like many employers, had to lower salaries. The salaries of both teachers were lowered again in March 1933. They were then making less than they had in 1926. Nevertheless, both continued to work in the school.

In view of these hardships, it is perhaps surprising to find that Marymount did take on some major projects during the early 1930s. However, one

Chapter Three:
THE THIRTIES
THE GREAT
DEPRESSION AND
EXPANSION

School ledger, 1934-35

room overlooking Fifth Avenue. The altar was donated by the Byrne family, whose four daughters attended the school. The former chapel became the students' dining room.

In the summer of 1932, Mother Ignatius left for Los Angeles and was succeeded by Mother Cecilia Rafter as superior. She was then replaced by Mother Therese Dalton in 1934.

In 1931, the beginnings of Marymount Manhattan College were emerging at Marymount Fifth Avenue, a testimony to the success of the school and the RSHM belief in higher education for women. In that year, in addition to junior school and high school, a junior college division was begun with four students, two of them Marymount high school graduates. They studied in the front room of the top floor of the 1028 building, a room that soon received the name "Siberia" because of its frigid temperatures resulting from its distance from the boiler.

In a decade when women such as Amelia Earhart, Jane Addams, and Frances Perkins were making their impact, Mother Butler established her own high expectations for Marymount students at all educational levels. The *Annals* of this first decade of Marymount's history give accounts of a rigorous curriculum including not only English, French, and social studies, but also Latin, mathematics, and science. A high school science club was formed, and despite the trend of the time to exclude classical languages from American high

suspects that in 1930 people did not expect the Depression to last so long or to be so devastating. Moreover, some of the costs Marymount incurred were offset by a number of donations. In March 1930, Mother Butler visited the school and decided to transfer the chapel to the location of the reception

Science Club

1931

Amelia Earhart is the first woman to make a solo flight across the Atlantic	Jane Addams of Hull House is the first woman to receive a Nobel Peace Prize

The first Hockey Club was officially organized in 1937.

school curricula, Marymount organized a classical club, called the Cicero Club. A Glee Club was also formed. School traditions continued to flourish. High school pins with the school symbol and motto *"Spes, Salus, Consolatio Nostra"* ("Our Hope, Health and Comfort") became available in the 1931-32 school year. The first tea dance, with 200 guests, was held on December 28, 1933, and the placement of the annual Christmas tree in the foyer first appeared in 1936. The first three-day retreat was conducted in February 1932. The first meeting of the Alumnae Association was November 15, 1935. The Mothers' Auxiliary was established in 1936, the year of Marymount's 10th anniversary.

Ping Pong tournaments rounded out the school's athletic program in 1937

It was also in 1936, on May 30th, that Cardinal Hayes gave Mother Butler permission to purchase the 1027 building, the Pratt Mansion, from Herbert Lee Pratt, a former president of Standard Oil Company. In view of the fact that the school's income the preceding year had reached the lowest point since the school opened, in hindsight the risk seems extraordinary. However, it appears that Mother Butler, expecting the school's enrollment to grow and its programs to expand, possessed the vision and courage to obtain the neighboring building when it came up for sale. The expansion also allowed for the official formation of the junior college division. It is in September 1936 that one finds mention of "the first freshman class [10 students] of the new Marymount Junior College." This reference agrees with Marymount Manhattan College's accepted date of founding as 1936.

Correspondence regarding the renovations to the Pratt building indicates that Mr. James Burns of Cross and Brown Real Estate, a Butler family friend, was helpful with the renovation planning. Other firms involved in the renovations were Rogan and Rogan, attorneys, and Schwartz and Gross, architects. At this time, Mother Butler was travelling, visiting the European houses. It is interesting to see how the RSHM in New York communicated with her, specifying on which ship they were sending the letters: "I am sending off all these answers on the NOR-MANDIE." "All your other questions I shall try and answer and send on the BREMEN tomorrow." The letters, sent from Marymount College, Tarrytown, refer to going down to Fifth Avenue to check on the renovations and are replete with references to the location of rooms, heating, wiring and lighting, plastering, painting and staining, and furnishings and curtains.

1932
Franklin D. Roosevelt is elected to his first term as President

1933
Frances Perkins becomes the first woman Secretary of Labor and Cabinet Member

Second floor Foyer, currently library computer research area

The Entrance Hall

1933
*New Deal laws are
passed to promote
economic recovery*

1937
*The Hindenburg
explodes at
Lakehurst, NJ*

The Music Salon, currently the Alumnae Parlor

The Walnut Room, currently library/technology rooms

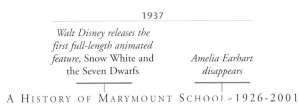

1937

Walt Disney releases the first full-length animated feature, Snow White and the Seven Dwarfs

Amelia Earhart disappears

Reading through these letters makes clear that they called the room on the first floor of 1027, now the Alumnae Parlor, "The Music Salon." "The Walnut Room" on the second floor, now divided into the library and the technology rooms, was also the front of the chapel at one point in time. "The American Room" on the third floor became the auditorium, as it is today. It was so named because it was completely paneled in American hardwoods.

Creating passages between the two buildings was the most challenging aspect of the renovation, especially because of the different heights of the floor levels between 1027 and 1028. The original thought was to have one cut-through on the third floor, but the RSHM became concerned about having to walk up to the third floor every time they wanted to pass through to the other building. They then looked at creating an additional cut-through on the first floor, either by removing two bathrooms to create a hallway or by connecting the 1028 library to the 1027 Music Salon, which might disrupt the activities housed in those two rooms. The sisters made a diagram, labeled the first option "A" and the second "B," and asked Mother Butler to cable her preference. The cut-through on the third floor became option "C." Seemingly, both the "A" plan and the "C" plan were chosen. The "C" plan was modified to cut through a closet rather than through what was then the kindergarten room at the front of the third floor.

It is also clear that additional connections on the ground floor and on the roof were made. The roof connection afforded a larger play area for the younger students. In fact, before any connections between the buildings were made, the RSHM developed an interesting strategy for getting from one building to the next without having to use the street entrances. They placed a ladder between the two roofs and climbed across.

Tea Dance 1938

TIME:
Monday, December 27, 1938
4:00-6:30

PLACE:
The Waldorf Astoria

SETTING:
The Empire Room

MUSIC AND LYRICS:
Xavier Cugat

PRODUCERS:
Mothers of
Marymount students

DIRECTRESS:
Miss Virginia Dunne

ASSISTANT DIRECTRESS:
Miss Carolyn Feldmann

COSTUMES:
Shops of Fifth Avenue

BOX OFFICE RECEIPTS:
Over the top

Tea Dance Committee, 1938

The fire code also required fire doors at these cut-throughs. The one on the first floor is a metal door that drops down from the top. It is still there, in the passage between 1028 and 1027. The addition of 1027 gave Marymount School additional classrooms for the junior college and high school, an auditorium, a new dining room and art studio, another classroom, and a science laboratory.

1938
Germany annexes
Austria

1939
Britain and France
declare war on
Germany

Activities A to Z

(Excerpts from Marifia, *1936)*

A: Arrivals at Marymount of old and new comers after the long vacation, to begin a new school year.

B: Bridge Party. The first social event of its kind organized by the Marymount Fifth Avenue Alumnae was held at the school on January 23.

C: Children of Mary. The Seniors had the privilege of being received into the Sodality of the Children of Mary, while the Juniors and Sophomores had the happiness of becoming aspirants.

D: Debates. The Seniors and Juniors debated the following question: Resolved: That the American press should be strictly censored.

E: Exhibition in Foyer of unique Bronze Crucifix executed by Cellini. Its records indicate that it belonged in 1600 to Cardinal Guadagni.

F: Feast Day of Reverend Mother, October 3. A day of general rejoicing.

G: Graduation. The Commencement Exercises took place on May 29. Marymount was singularly happy in having his Eminence Patrick Cardinal Hayes, Archbishop of New York, to preside.

H: Hallow'een was celebrated by an informal luncheon, complete with the orange and black of the day. The Junior School, as usual, outdid themselves in variety and ingenuity of colorful costumes.

I: In memory of First Communion Day. This, the most dignified of all ceremonies, was carried out in solemn French fashion this year. The little girls in their white ankle-length dresses and the little boys in their smart uniform suits left a deep impression on all by their recollected attitude.

J: Junior Museum Course. The Juniors attended a series of Gallery Talks at the Metropolitan Museum of Art. Decorative Arts, Glass, Silver, and Ceramics were discussed.

K: Keen activity was "en evidence" when the oils, water colors, pastels, pen-and-ink sketches, fashion illustrations and drawings from casts were transferred from the Studio for the Parents' Day Exhibition to the library.

L: Lecture delivered by Mr. Maurice Leahy, noted English lecturer, author, and founder of the Catholic Poetry Society, London.

M: Midnight Mass in the Convent Chapel, at which some of us had the privilege of assisting.

N: Novel Course, of an informal nature, was started this year, and included the reading of well-known dramas. Barrie, Milne and Tarkington were our favorites.

O: On Retreat, given by Father Charles Gallagher, S. J. Two days were given over to recollection and prayer.

P: Present Fashion Show, featuring the present and coming styles for the well-dressed "debs" and tiny tots. A popular innovation with us, and one, we think, which has come to stay.

Q: "Quality Street" presented by our Dramatic Club on December 15, the proceeds of which were devoted to Christmas charities.

R: Reverend Mother General's Feast Day. A programme largely in French, welcomed Reverend Mother General when she came to celebrate her feast this year on the Patronage of St. Joseph.

S: Surprise Tea was given in the Blue Room for the members of the Tea Dance Committee.

T: Theater Parties. In connection with the newly organized Drama-Reading Club Group, Lou Ellen Creamer was elected Chairman. Some of the plays visited were "Pride and Prejudice," "Libel," and "Victoria Regina."

U: Unique Parents' Day Programme, in which the Junior School gave a delightful display of dancing in the playlet, "The International Bouquet."

V: Visit of Bishop Bernard. As a result of his interesting talk we became fired with missionary zeal, proceeded to collect money and donate a quantity of much-needed material to his needy missionaries in the Bahamas.

W: Washington's Birthday had its own place on the school curriculum. The classes were represented individually in patriotic poems and plays.

X: Xmas Charities. Many baskets were filled for the poor, while a bazaar was held on the day of the play. Proceeds of both were devoted to charity.

Y: Yearly Dance held at the Central Park Casino proved a social and financial success.

Z: Zeal was shown in many school activities during the year, notably in the debates and play-reading groups. Notable activity was shown in mission work, social functions, and in floral presentations to the Chapel.

1939
*Spanish Civil War
ends*

1940
Battle of Britain

Alumnae Association

FROM THE EARLIEST years of the school graduates were encouraged to maintain bonds with the school and their former classmates and to visit often. A formal Alumnae Association was created on November 15, 1935. At this inaugural meeting, Mary Rita Byrne '31 was elected the first president and Rita Horton '31 was elected treasurer. A calendar of social events was drawn up that included a bridge party and communion breakfast. An Annual Luncheon and Bridge at Sherry's was initiated, hosted jointly by the alumnae and the Mothers' Auxiliary.

Interest in the Association waned during World War II, when world events took precedence in the lives of Marymount alumnae. After the war, with the support of Reverend Mother Rita Rowley and Mother Majella Berg, the group was revived. The college alumnae and the school alumnae were divided into two groups in 1948, when the junior college was ready to move into its new building. The school's many alumnae continued to reunite during the 1950s, and nearly seventy graduates attended a Holy Hour on December 28, 1959.

While occasional meetings of alumnae were held during the 1960s, a desire for the Alumnae Association to be reorganized on a more formal basis was expressed at the end of the decade by both alumnae and the newly formed Board of Trustees. The December 1969 minutes of the Board note that both alumnae and student representatives "may be invited to attend specific Board meetings." In September of 1975, the president of the Alumnae Association became an *ex-officio* member of the Board of Trustees. Mary Jane McCabe Belt '58 was the first alumna to hold this position.

During the 1970s, the senior seminar and internship programs were begun, bringing graduating students and alumnae from many professions together and helping those same students find internships in May of their senior year. Alumnae also instituted a yearly phonathon to support the Annual Fund. By 1988, they were actively involved in the school's capital campaign and established a faculty endowment plan in the name of Sister Antoine Campbell.

During the 1990s, the Alumnae Association began new programs to encourage alumnae to return to the school and become more involved. Introduced during that decade were trips to museums and botanical gardens, lectures on art, health, and finance, and regional events in Boston, Florida, and Washington.

During 2001, Marymount's 75th Anniversary year, alumnae from all over the world returned to the school in record numbers. That year marked the first three-day Alumnae Reunion and the publication of the first Alumnae Directory. In 2001, the Association also redefined the

Reunion 2000, Class of 1950

Alumnae Association class agents, June 2001 end-of-year reception

*Lou Ellen Creamer '36, the first student to enter the school
in 1926, is given a painting of the school door by
Dr. Jane Haher-Izquierdo '58, President of the Board of Trustees
and the artist at the 1996 Alumnae Reunion.*

term *alumna* to include not only graduates, but any student who attended Marymount at any level. As a result, Marymount recognized male alumni from the early childhood program.

Today, the Alumnae Association is an active, vibrant association led by a committed group of class agents and other volunteers and assisted by the Director of Alumnae Relations. The Alumnae Association has an exciting, varied program of activities, ranging from seminars and lectures to festive holiday parties, homecomings, and reunions and regional events. The Association helps alumnae network with peers and maintain the bonds formed during their school days. Alumnae hold major leadership positions in the governance of the school, are active members of the Board of Trustees, and are strong financial supporters. Alumnae give generously of their time and talent, and their recollections and memorabilia continue to enrich Marymount's historical archives.

As Marymount looks ahead, the alumnae are a reflection of Mother Butler's spirit—a link to the past and a key to the future.

*Here, in this school
where once their voices rang
And in this chapel
where child-voices sang,
The busy traffic
of the world must cease,
Yielding tranquility
and heavenly peace.
Alumnae pause,
there in the lamp's soft glow,
Recapturing memories
of years ago.
And in their hearts
rise the eager fount
Of loyalty and love for
Marymount.*

MARIFIA, *1936*

Parents' Association

IN MARCH 1936, during the 10th Anniversary year, the Marymount School Mothers' Auxiliary was founded.

The *Annals* relate that early in the 1930s, the mothers started a Sewing Guild which aided the St. Vincent de Paul Society. The Mothers' Auxiliary of the time supported the scholarship fund and organized the parent-daughter communion breakfasts that "helped form strong liaisons between parents and faculty." They formed the Mother Butler Guild that "concentrated on providing First Communion outfits and vestments for home and foreign missions." Marymount Fifth Avenue mothers worked with the Marymount College mothers on dinner dances to benefit the scholarship fund.

At the same time, there was a Fathers' Association, which was responsible for the capital improvements at the school. In the 1950s and 1960s, according to the *Annals,* "the fathers re-equipped the biology laboratory, the library, the reading room, the large reception room in 1027, and the teahouse." In 1962, the auditorium was renovated by the fathers to include paneling the walls, upgrading the stage, and providing new drapes, stage curtains, and lights. The fathers also donated chandeliers, rugs, and furnishings for the chapel as well as other kinds of equipment. In addition to various development projects, the Fathers' Association served the important task of connecting Marymount School to corporate resources.

When the school governance was transferred to a Board of Trustees in 1969, the organization of a parents' association was discussed by the Board. On May 18, 1970, it was decided that a new Parents' Association would include both mothers and fathers and would be involved in finance/development work and communications between the school and parents. In 1975, the president of the Parents' Association became an *ex-officio* member of the Board of Trustees for the length of his/her term.

Annette Hayde, who was president of the Parents' Association from 1981 to 1983, recalls two of the then-new events that have become so much a part of Marymount culture. One is Grandparents' Day (started in 1983, now designated Grandparents' and Special Friends' Day). Another is the auction, the first of which took place in 1983. At the time, the Parents' Association was seeking a fundraising event that would attract a broad range of parents, alumnae, and friends. Mrs. Hayde recalls,"The Board agreed to try an auction as an alternative to the annual black-tie dinner dance traditionally held at a hotel or private club. We kept the black-tie event but held the benefit at the school. Mr. Bill Doyle of the William Doyle Galleries conducted the auction. The evening was very successful as both a financial and social event, and continues today as a part of the annual Spring Gala."

1957

1976

PARENTS' ASSOCIATION LEADERSHIP THROUGH THE YEARS

The role of the Parents' Association has evolved but remains tied to its roots of providing support to the school community. Mothers and fathers still provide development support through various PA-sponsored events, foster open communication between the school and the parent body, and even sew costumes for the many pageants and productions in which the students participate. The scope of many Parents' Association events has grown with the school.

The most recent Spring Benefit Gala celebrated Marymount's seventy-five years with the participation of more than 500 parents, faculty, alumnae, and friends of the school. Parents' Association communication efforts include pages on the school Web site as well as the more traditional "phone chain" and general meetings. Parents' Association support now covers areas as diverse as video editing and graphic design, sponsoring cultural and business internships, and career panels for seniors. The Parents' Association fully believes in the words of Headmistress Kathleen Fagan that "when parents are involved in the school, it sends the message to their daughters that school is important!"

2001

"Our mothers have become identified with the work of the school, of the Church and of Catholic education."

ANNALS, *1936*

"A Bridge and Tea held in the Foyer proved a very pleasant function at which our guests made many new friends, and during which they were entertained by a highly classical musical programme of harp and vocal selections by concert artists."

MARIFIA, *1936*

Junior School students during the 1940s consult a map of World War I in an effort to better understand the events of World War II.

HE YEARS surrounding the turn of the decade were tumultuous ones: the Second World War began in 1939, and in the same year, the church experienced the death of Pius XI and the election of Pius XII and, in New York, the appointment of Francis Cardinal Spellman as Archbishop. In 1940, Marymount experienced its own personal tragedy with the death of Mother Butler at Tarrytown.

In the last years of her life, despite her age and illness, and the upheaval in Europe, Mother Butler had made several ocean voyages to visit the RSHM European communities and to meet with Pope Pius XII, who agreed to remain the "Protector" of the Institute. Even in the last months of her life when she could no longer travel from Tarrytown, Mother Butler kept in close touch with news from around the Institute and was especially concerned about the wartime dangers experienced by the RSHM in Europe.

After Mother Butler's death, Mother Therese Dalton was transferred to Tarrytown, and Mother Immaculée McMullen came to Fifth Avenue as superior. Mother Raymunde McKay served as principal of the high school from 1943 to 1953.

The *Annals* and the *Marifia* editions from these years suggest that Marymount students were quite involved in war-related activities and issues. Debate topics concerned whether "a high school girl should go on to college or into war work," and whether "the United States should relieve the distress of occupied areas by shipments of food and other necessities." The Current Events Club tracked war news. With the windows of The Metropolitan Museum of Art boarded up across the street, the junior college graduates of 1943 wrote in the *Marifia* with patriotic passion: "From our college portals, we have witnessed the results of a barbaric endeavor to stifle Culture, but against the grim

Chapter Four:
THE WAR YEARS

background of a Museum's boarded windows, our flag's 'bright stars' gleam with undimmed lustre." Social life also centered around the war, with junior college students hosting a holiday dinner dance for the officers of the British Navy and Saturday dances for young men of the army and navy. Air-raid practices were common, and aid packages were sent to both the Philippines and the European Rehabilitation Fund. Finally, since oil was needed for the war, Marymount converted its boilers back to coal for heat.

During World War II, space was also utilized in some unique ways. Marymount College students from Tarrytown sometimes stayed overnight on weekends since hotel reservations in the city were difficult to obtain. Portable beds were set up in classrooms on Friday nights. During the summers, overseas students from the college in Tarrytown boarded at Fifth Avenue. Obviously they could not return to Europe during the war. The RSHM community at Fifth Avenue helped care for a group of small children whose parents had escaped from countries in the war zone. Small numbers of students continued to board during the 1950s.

Field Hockey in Central Park, 1940

Debating Team of 1943 discusses whether high school graduates should go to college or into war work.

Students visiting The Metropolitan Museum of Art, 1941

First Communion in the school's chapel on the second floor of the 1028 building, 1943

1941		1943	
Japanese attack Pearl Harbor; U.S. enters World War II	*1942 Womens' military services established*	*Withholding tax on wages is introduced*	*Income Tax is levied*

Sister Raymunde McKay, RSHM
At Marymount School 1941-1953

BORN IN LISBURN, Northern Ireland, Sister Raymunde McKay was educated locally by the Religious of the Sacred Heart of Mary. Sister Raymunde earned the Bachelor of Science degree in economics from the London School of Economics of the University of London. In 1934, she sailed to the United States and studied at Marymount, Tarrytown for two years prior to her profession into the order. After spending her first year teaching at Sacred Heart of Mary High School, Park Terrace, in upper Manhattan, she was transferred to Marymount School in 1941.

During her first years at Marymount, Sister Raymunde taught chemistry and supervised the music program. She was appointed principal in 1943, a position she held for ten years. During her tenure, Marymount School was chartered and accredited by the University of the State of New York, scholarship programs resulted in a more diverse student population, the 1026 building was acquired, and Marymount's impressive academic reputation grew. While spearheading all these developments, Sister Raymunde was also pursuing a Ph.D. in Economics from Fordham University. In 1953, Sister Raymunde left to become dean of Marymount College, 71st Street. During her years there,

the college became independent from Marymount College, Tarrytown, and on February 24, 1961, it received a charter from the Board of Regents of the State of New York as Marymount Manhattan College. Sister Raymunde served as its president.

In 1964, Sr. Raymunde traveled west to become president of Marymount College in Palos Verdes, California. She was pivotal in the merger of the College and the Jesuit Loyola University that became Loyola Marymount University in 1973.

In the mid-1970s, Sister Raymunde retired and traveled to Australia, Israel, and Russia. In 1981, she returned from her travels and became a member of the Board of Trustees of Loyola Marymount University. After celebrating her 50th Anniversary as an RSHM in 1986, she spent a year in Arlington, Virginia where she helped the college attain university status. In 1988, she returned to Marymount Manhattan College as interim president and then moved to England, where she served for a time at Marymount International School in Surrey.

Sister Raymunde is now retired and resides at the Marymount Convent in Tarrytown. Sister Raymunde can be well satisfied with her many years of educational leadership and vision, marked by a commitment to excellence in the education of women.

By KATHRYN I. TOOHIG '64

Sister Raymunde McKay

Upper School students, 1943

The junior class Christmas tea. Princess Alix of Luxembourg, a student during the war years, is pictured with the school pennant, Marifia, 1945.

Upper School students selling war bonds, 1945

1944		1945	
Allies land in Normandy	DNA is isolated by Oswald Avery	FDR dies and Harry Truman succeeds him	World War II ends

Students in Central Park, 1948

I
N THE YEARS after the war, Marymount's curriculum, extracurricular activities, and facilities all continued to grow. With Mother Immaculée McMullen's death in 1943, Mother Rita Rowley had come from Tarrytown to Marymount Fifth Avenue. With Mother Rita as superior and Mother Raymunde McKay as head of the school, Marymount enjoyed the leadership of two extraordinary educators. In 1946, the high school produced its first real school newspaper, the *Joritan*, the name a combination of Mother Joseph Butler and Mother Rita Rowley. Improvements in laboratory and library facilities were made. The uniform, which had been a one-piece dress, became a suit, and the *Annals* record that Marymount was the first Catholic school in the New York area to introduce a suit uniform.

The year 1946 was a pivotal one, for it was on June 21 that the school was chartered and accredited by the University of the State of New York. Despite the challenges of running three divisions – junior school, high school, and junior college – in the same facility, the school staff possessed impressive educational qualifications, advanced degrees, and excellent experience. Thus, the accreditation went so smoothly that after an unannounced visit, an inspector from the state determined that no subsequent formal visit was needed.

The international network of Marymount Schools also expanded in 1946 with the founding of Marymount International School in Rome. Founded in response to the need to educate international children living in Rome during the post-war years, it was expected to be a temporary school lasting only until the Allies left Italy. The school flourished, however, adding a boarding department two years later and moving from Via Nomentana to its present location on Via di Villa Lauchli in 1953. Via Nomentana remains the site of Istituto Marymount, the RSHM school accredited by the Italian government.

Chapter Five:
THE POST-WAR ERA
ACCREDITATION AND
NEW FOUNDATIONS

Science teacher, Mr. Campbell, with an Upper School physics class, c. 1947

The new uniform—a suit, 1946

Back at Marymount Fifth Avenue, expansion was also in progress. The junior college formally established in 1936 continued to grow during the 1940s. The number of junior college graduates increased steadily to 61 in 1948, the last year in which the junior college graduation was conducted from the 1027 building. In the 1947-48 school year, a building at 221 East 71st Street, formerly occupied by the Junior League, was acquired. The junior college moved to this site in 1948. Today it is known as Marymount Manhattan College. Mother Rita Rowley moved with the junior college and Mother du Carmel Connolly, who had taught at Marymount for twenty years, succeeded Mother Rita at Fifth Avenue as superior. Mother Raymunde McKay continued as head of the school.

The 1948-49 school year was also marked by the centenary celebrations of the founding of the Religious

1946
*United Nations
headquarters established
in New York City*

1947

*Marshall Plan aids
war-ravaged Europe*

*United Nations
announces plan to
partition Israel*

44   A HISTORY OF MARYMOUNT SCHOOL~1926-2001

Junior School student at the end of the day, 1948

Junior School students model in the fashion show.

Junior School students entering the dining room on the second floor of the 1027 building.
All students were expected to curtsy whenever they met one of their teachers.

of the Sacred Heart of Mary. Centennial medals were distributed to students on February 24th, Gailhac scholarships were awarded, and various contests were conducted among students in RSHM schools. The *Marifia* was dedicated to the RSHM.

Meanwhile, the Alumnae Association, which had become less active during the war years, was revived in 1945. Among their principal activities were an annual Communion Breakfast and a party for children in Goldwater Memorial Hospital. An annual fashion show was reestablished in 1947 and a tea dance in 1948. Although the college and high school alumnae had shared one association since 1938, the two organizations were separated after the junior college moved to the 71st Street building.

Christmas performance

Christmas dance

Students preparing packages for war relief

Junior School science

1948
Columbia Records introduces the 33 1/3 RPM LP record

1949
Harvard Law School begins admitting women

United Nations recognizes Israel as a nation

46   A HISTORY OF MARYMOUNT SCHOOL~1926-2001

Mother Rita Rowley, RSHM (1913-1963) At Marymount School 1943-1948

BORN IN IRELAND in 1913, Mother Rita Rowley entered the Religious of the Sacred Heart of Mary in 1931 at Tarrytown. Subsequently, she studied at the Sorbonne in Paris, received a Master's Degree from McGill University, Montreal, and a Ph.D. from Laval University, Quebec, Canada.

As an educational and religious leader, Mother Rita's influence was profound. Coming to Marymount School Fifth Avenue from Tarrytown in 1943, Mother Rita served as superior of the religious community and head of the school until 1948. In collaboration with Sister Raymunde McKay, Mother Rita played a pivotal role in securing Marymount's charter and accreditation by the University of the State of New York, establishing Marymount's position as a highly respected academic institution.

In 1948, Mother Rita left Marymount School to become dean of the new Marymount College (New York City) when it moved from the 1027 building at Fifth Avenue to its new site on 71st Street. In 1953, Mother Rita became superior of the religious community at Marymount College, Tarrytown, and in 1959, she was named RSHM Provincial of the Eastern North American Province. A year later, she was elected General Superior of the entire order.

Mother Rita served as the seventh General Superior of the Religious of the Sacred Heart of Mary for only three years, until her death on July 1, 1963, but it was she who guided the Institute through the changes brought by the Second Vatican Council, ensured that every province would have representation at the general level, and expanded the educational and other ministries of the order. Mother Rita is buried in the crypt beneath the Butler Memorial Chapel at the Marymount Convent in Tarrytown.

Traditional morning welcome at Marymount School

I N 1950, the year before Marymount's silver anniversary, continued expansion resulted in the acquisition of the Dunlevy Milbank Mansion at 1026 Fifth Avenue. Even though the junior college had moved to its own site, additional space was needed for the growing academic program from pre-kindergarten through the high school. Accounts of repairs, alterations, inspections, new boilers, and a new chimney fill the *Annals*. The chapel was moved from the 1028 building and expanded to twice its size spanning the front of the 1026 and 1027 buildings. A permanent certificate of occupancy for 1026 was acquired on March 11, 1952.

Two years later, however, on April 14, 1954, disaster struck the 1026 building and a tragedy was narrowly averted. The building next door, at 1025 Fifth Avenue, was being torn down to make way for a new apartment house. In the process, a massive chimney collapsed and hit the south wall of 1026, tearing a ten-foot hole through the wall of a fifth-floor classroom. The entire building shook. The accident occurred on the Wednesday of Holy Week. School was immediately closed for Easter vacation, and when students returned, classes resumed using every available space in the 1027-28 buildings until repairs could be completed. Today, there are two windows in the south wall where the wall was struck, and some alumnae never look up there without thinking of that April day.

It was during the 1950s that the Fathers' Association at Marymount took a leadership role in development activities. On January 8, 1957, the new biology laboratory, the result of the generosity of Mrs. Stratford Wallace and the Fathers' Association, was dedicated in memory of Dr. Stratford Wallace. On February 24, 1958, the new library in memory of Mrs. John A. Mullen, created in conjunction with efforts by the Fathers' Association, was dedicated.

Chapter Six: THE FIFTIES CONTINUED EXPANSION

Consolidation of the three buildings, 1950

the American Association of French Teachers, the *Auxilium Latinum,* the Catholic Classical Association, the Hearst American History Contest, National Catholic Science Council, and the New York *Journal American.* Then as now, academic curriculum was complemented by lessons on values and conduct.

Guest speakers, RSHM, various priests, and others, were frequent visitors at Marymount during these years. They often spoke on religious topics or about the missions. For example, the 1955-56 school year included a visit by Mother du Sacre Coeur Smith, president of Marymount College, Tarrytown, who came to show movies of RSHM working in missions in Mozambique and Rhodesia (now Zimbabwe). In 1956, Marymount

While the facilities were enhanced, the educational program was growing under new leadership. In 1954, Mother du Carmel Connolly was transferred to Tarrytown, and Mother Winifred McConville was named Mother Superior. She was assisted by Mother Antoine Campbell, who had become principal of the high school the previous year and who served in that position until 1965. Junior School principals in the 1950s were Mother des Anges Bennett and Mother Timothy Fahey.

Academic excellence continued to be a hallmark of a Marymount education. During the 1949-50 school year, the school came in fourth out of 238 high schools in the first mathematics contest sponsored by the New York Metropolitan Section of the Mathematical Association of America. (The first three schools were Bronx High School of Science, Brooklyn Technical High School, and Abraham Lincoln High School, Brooklyn.) Two years later, the school came in third in this contest, in which 2,000 students participated. Students were also successful in various other competitions sponsored by

When the mansion at 1025 was demolished the south wall of the 1026 building was damaged

1950
Senator Joseph McCarthy warns against Communists in the State Department

U.S. sends advisors to Vietnam

1951
Korean conflict begins

Glee Club, Class of 1950 and others

Dedication of the new library, 1958

school levels; dramatic club productions and operettas, most notably *Amahl and the Night Visitors,* directed by Mother Leo McKallagat; parent-daughter Communion breakfasts and father-daughter square dances; two-day retreats in school and weekend retreats at Cormaria Retreat House, Sag Harbor; reception into the Children of Mary Sodality for the high school and First Communions, Confirmations and May processions with the crowning of Mary for the Junior School. During these years, commencement was held annually

Dedication of the new biology lab, 1957

Fathers' Association dinner held on the second floor of the 1027 building

in Umtali, Rhodesia, opened. Two RSHM from Marymount Fifth Avenue, Mother Claver Kelly and Mother des Anges Bennett, were later transferred to Rhodesia and, on return visits, brought wonderfully informative stories.

Marymount's annual traditions and events flourished throughout the 1950s. The *Annals* recount a whole host of activities, with proceeds from fundraising events supporting a variety of charities. There were Christmas Cantatas and Christmas formal dances; fashion shows at both the junior school and high

1951
UNIVAC (Universal
Automatic Computer)
is introduced

1952

Jonas Salk develops
the polio vaccine

Queen Elizabeth II
is crowned

A HISTORY OF MARYMOUNT SCHOOL ~ 1926-2001   51

Junior School outing to the Bronx Zoo

in the Great Hall of Marymount 71st Street. School publications won awards from the Columbia Press Association and the Marquette League. At the same time, activities that were considered so time-consuming that they detracted from academic work were curtailed. For example, the annual song contest was discontinued in 1958.

Students of the 1950s were also actively engaged in social-service work. Besides making contributions to various charities, they sewed for the missions, held food and clothing drives, taught Confraternity of Christian Doctrine classes (religious education for public-school students), and did social-service projects at the Helpers of the Holy Souls or Carmelite Home for the Aged.

The Mothers' Auxiliary and Fathers' Association were both increasingly active during these years. In addition to contributions to the building and to sponsoring student events, they both held their own social and religious events: annual Holy Hours (an hour designated for special prayer), the Mothers' Auxiliary Annual Bridge and Tea, and, the Fathers' Association President's Reception. The end of the fifties was marked by the death of Pope Pius XII and the election of Pope John XXIII in 1958, and by the death of Mother Gerard Phelan and election of Mother Rita Rowley as the seventh General Superior of the Religious of the Sacred Heart of Mary in 1960. At Marymount, Mother Berchmans Walsh replaced Mother Winifred McConville as superior in the same year.

Marymount School transportation, 1954

Students from Classes 1953 and 1954 during a typing class

1952

Dwight D. Eisenhower is elected President

Watson and Crick discover DNA structure

The Second Sex by Simone DeBeauvoir states feminist views

"Notes." Students and faculty assembled and each student's grades were read aloud. Certificates of honor were also presented. (Upper School "Notes" above, Junior School "Notes" below), 1958 Marifia

The Sacrament of Confirmation, c. 1950

Students after their induction into the Sodality of the Children of Mary, December 1955

1954

The Supreme Court bans racial segregation in public schools

Tennessee William's Cat on a Hot Tin Roof opens on Broadway

Sister Antoine Campbell, RSHM (1909-1998)
At Marymount School 1929-1936, 1953-1966, 1968-1991

Sister Antoine Campbell (center), with Jane Haher-Izquierdo '58 (on left), Sister Kathleen Fagan '59 and Cathy Sattenstein Callender '60 (on right).

Fifth Avenue, as head of the high school, and she also taught speech to all students. She left Fifth Avenue in 1966 to serve as Reverend Mother at Marymount Quebec and then at Marymount in Rome. In 1968, she returned to Fifth Avenue as a Latin teacher and alumnae director.

Fond memories and stories of Sister Antoine abound. Although she projected a rather austere presence, she had a marvelous sense of humor. The combination of her demeanor and distinctive speaking voice made her a perfect candidate for amateur comedians and mimics, and there was at least one in every class. Sister Antoine took it well. Later I came back to work with Sister

BORN IN DUNDALK, Ireland on July 9, 1909, Sister Antoine Campbell was the niece of Sister Ignatius Kearney. She entered the Religious of the Sacred Heart of Mary in Tarrytown in 1926, and came to Marymount Fifth Avenue in 1929 as a Latin and history teacher and remained until 1936. She spent the next sixteen years of her teaching career at Sacred Heart of Mary and St. Thomas Aquinas schools, both in the Bronx, New York.

In 1953 she was reassigned to Marymount School

Antoine in the Development office. Little did I think, back in the early '60s, that I would one day be working side-by-side with one of the most formidable authority figures of my youth. Let's face it. First impressions of Sister Antoine, especially to a fourteen-year-old, were daunting. It wasn't until one made it through first and second "forms" that she let you in on the fact that she had a great sense of humor.

Sister Antoine's dedication to the school and its needs knew no bounds, and she gladly volunteered every night of the annual phonathon. She had a special group of people, alumnae and alumnae parents, whom she liked to call. Though a rather shy person in many ways, she had great courage when it came to asking for anything for Marymount School. There is a story that after one night of phoning, she was back at work calling first thing in the morning. Her first call that day was to an alumna in Los Angeles who was awakened by the distinctive voice of Sister Antoine. The alumna was more than willing to give. She must have been alarmed at the urgency of Marymount's needs, since the call was made at 9 a.m. New York time, 6 a.m. California time!

In April 1978, Marymount School honored Sister Antoine on her 50th jubilee as an RSHM. The event was a great celebration and evidence of the loving affection so many felt for her. The program that day included a Mass and some very touching speeches. In addition, Ann Scavullo, class of 1963, wrote a song in Sister Antoine's honor to the tune of "Ascot Opening Day" from *My Fair Lady*. She also sang the song, dressed in her old school uniform—tam, white gloves, and all.

Sister Antoine retired to the Marymount Convent in Tarrytown in 1991. She died on March 13, 1998.

At the time of her memorial service, a former student remembered Sister Antoine:

"Of course, she will always be Mother Antoine to our generation, aloof yet accessible, strict but with that smile that was always possible and, when given, so captivating; we knew she loved us even when our knees were knocking. How elegantly she made the transition from habit and all it represented to the trim, efficient, and triumphantly retro lady who symbolized Marymount tradition. Strength, dignity, calm—rough edges became smooth in her presence. I hope she thinks of us fondly as we muddle along, and keeps a place up there for each of us close to her watchful eye so we don't embarrass her when we clamber in."

(The Honorable Katherine Jackson Hayden '59)

By KATHLEEN O'SHEA DONOHUE '63

Sister Antoine with Kathleen Harshberger,
Chair of the 60th Anniversary celebration

Sister Antoine with Reverend George McMahon, S.J.

Senior religion classes taught by Jesuit priests. Above, Class of 1958, below, Class of 1959

Song Contest: A group of juniors from the Class of '59 celebrating having won the cherished award. Song Contest was one of the first activities of the year. Each class wrote, directed, produced, and performed an original skit. "If we think back on it, we can see how, in our first year here, we were not quite acclimated and had hardly any idea of what class spirit was, much less the Song Contest. But in a few short weeks, what began as a mere group of girls became a united class, struggling for all it was worth to win a contest it had never heard of before. There, all at once, was the beginning of Class Spirit, that 'Je ne sais quoi' that was so terribly important in the later months." (Susan O'Leary '57 Joritan, *November 1956) Song Contest ended in the late 1950s, but there may be remnants remaining in the current custom of Halloween skits.*

"Our teachers steered us toward curiosity, creativity, and excitement about intellectual pursuits. I learned that when people are treated with respect and love, they can thrive and they can be joyful. That's why Marymount has my heart, my loyalty and my deep gratitude."

Catherine Hohenlohe Jacobus '60

1955

Rosa Park refuses to give up her seat – Montgomery Bus Boycott follows

U.S. and Soviet Union plan to launch earth satellites

Picasso exhibit opens in Paris

Students collecting for the Red Cross,
Cardinal Spellman contributing to their cause

Father-Daughter Square Dance, c. 1959. Piute Pete,
of the Village Barn, pictured in overalls, was the caller for many years.

Mothers' Tea, 1958

Annual Parent-Daughter Communion Breakfast, held in
the dining room on the second floor of the 1027 building, 1952

A Choral Club production of Amahl and the Night Visitors, 1954

1957
Russia lauches
Sputnik

1958
European Common
Market is established

A HISTORY OF MARYMOUNT SCHOOL · 1926-2001

57

Upper School students entering the school buildings
appropriately attired complete with tams and white gloves. There were
strict rules in the 1950s about wearing the required hat and gloves
to and from school.

School uniforms, 1959

A 1954 Fashion Show
held in the school's auditorium

Christmas Prom, Classes of '56 and '57

1958

School desegregation
runs into strong
opposition

President Eisenhower
sends troops to
Little Rock

*Junior School students walking in Central Park
with their teachers after lunch.*

Dodge-ball in Central Park, 1955

*Team captains discuss plans with Miss Cody, Director of Athletics.
"Volleyball and basketball tournaments head the list in this year's
sports calendar." Marifia, 1950*

*A rooftop basketball game. The addition of the 1026 building in
1950 gave students an uninterrupted space to practice team sports.*

Marymount Boys

LTHOUGH Marymount is known as a school for girls, small numbers of boys have been enrolled during the last seventy-five years, many times because they had a sister already attending the school. The grandsons of James Butler were among the first thirteen students to walk in the door in February of 1926, and there was an all-boy class named after St. Stanislaus in the 1920s. Boys may not have been enrolled during times when the school was filled to capacity. In 1950, to coincide with the purchase of the Dunlevy Milbank Mansion, there was an announcement that the school would again have the space to be able to enroll boys. Boys were only in the youngest grades, and left by the first or second grade to attend boys' schools in the neighborhood.

Today, boys attend only the nursery and pre-kindergarten classes. Two Marymount boys from earlier years have returned to their first school, one as a faculty member (Colm McMahon), the other as a parent of a Marymount student. The following story was written by that parent.

A Marymount Boy's Story

The three buildings on the corner of Fifth Avenue and 84th Street that are home to Marymount School of New York are sentimental personal landmarks for me. It was there more than forty-five years ago that I began my formal education in academics and religion as well as etiquette and manners. "Marymount Fifth Avenue," as it was called during my years of attendance, was one of the most prominent Catholic girls' schools in New York, a status the school enjoys today. Frequently, people will remark: "You're a guy and Marymount is a girls' school. How did you go there?" The fact is that Marymount New York has, during most of its history, provided places in the early childhood years for boys like me who were brothers of Marymount students. My sister, Hope, was in the Class of 1959.

I have special memories of my first school. I learned the basics of reading, mathematics, and science as well as some very useful practical skills such as how to tell time. I remember catechism class, which prepared me for my first communion in the school chapel. It was a wonderful learning, social, and religious experience that I never forgot.

Our daughter Kayle was born on my birthday, prompting my wife, Kathy, to say: "She will be just like you!" When the time came three years ago to choose a nursery school for Kayle, one of my first thoughts was Marymount because if there was one way that I wanted

my daughter to be like me it was to have the benefit of starting school at Marymount. I knew that once my wife walked into the school she would share with me great affection for the old and the new Marymount. We felt welcomed as part of the extended Marymount family and were as impressed with the modern changes as well as the ongoing moral and religious traditions of the school. Without losing any of its character, Marymount has indeed moved forward with the times, especially in areas such as computer technology.

I rediscovered a school that made me immensely proud. I told all who would listen that I was at Marymount in the 1950s and remembered the portrait of Mother Butler in the library, and how the tables at lunch were graded for manners. Kathy and Kayle both said how much they liked my school.

We are immensely gratified that Kayle is the third generation of our family to attend Marymount. Almost every time I walk up the famous spiral stairs at the school with Kayle, more memories of those young years return to me. I wonder how many other Marymount boys became Marymount fathers. All of them must have been as overjoyed as I am to see their daughters flourish in their first school. Now Marymount is once again one of the most important and rewarding parts of my family's life.

By JOHN CROSSON, father of Kayle '13

Three young boys practice their bows

John Crosson (center), during an outing to Central Park, 1958 Marifia.

A musical band in the 1930s

Boys and girls learn together in a classroom, 1952.

Daily Record of *Marymount*

(*2nd* Term of School Year)

No.	PUPILS' NAMES Classe de l'Enfant Jesus	Age	M T W T F M T W T F M T W T F M T
1	Junior Broderick		a a a x x x x x x x x x x a a
2	Timmy Healy		x x a x x x x x x x x x x a a
3	Grover Whalen		x x x x x x x x x x x x x x
4	John Ryan		x x x x x x x x x x x x x x x x
5	Walter Travers		x x x a a u a a x a x x a x
6	Richard Keating		x x x x x x x x x x x x x x x
7	Harry Balfe		a a a x x x x x x x x x x x
8	Robert White		x x x x x x x x x x x x x x
9	Albert Keller		a a a a a a a x x x x x x x
10	Mary D dos Passos		a a a x x x x x x a a a a x x
11	Patricia Ryan		x x x x x x x x x x x x x x
8)12	Marillyn Miller		x x x x x a x x x x x x x x x
13	Ann Clark		a x x x x x x x a a a a a a u
14	Audrey C Magee		x x x x x x x x x x x x x x x x
15	Barbara Ridder		a a a a a a a a a a a a a a
16	Mary Gentile		x x x x x x x x x x x x x x x
17	Mary U Travers		x x x x x x x x a a a a a a u
18	Dorothy Burghard		x x x x x x x x x x x x a a w x

Daily Record, 1927, showing Classe de l'Enfant Jesus that included Timmy Healy, later Reverend Timothy S. Healy, S.J., President, Georgetown University, 1977-89, President of the New York Public Library, 1989-92.

The old clock and the new uniforms . . . Campbell tartan skirts and charcoal-gray blazers, Fall 1961

M ARYMOUNT IN the 1960s was an interesting combination of traditional customs and attitudes and the emerging ideas that reflected the changes sweeping the church and the world. By the end of the decade, Marymount had evolved into a school that seemed quite different from the school of the early 1960s.

Many traditions were reviewed in light of enormous social, cultural, and religious change in society. Mission Club activities, Sodality, the Christmas Dance, the Father-Daughter Square Dance, the Junior-Senior Tea, the Graduates and Parents Ball, and the Senior-Faculty dinner all endured.

The Mothers' Auxiliary and the Fathers' Association also continued to be very active. While the mothers' group focused on mission work and fund-raising through social events such as the Bridge, Tea and Fashion Show, the fathers did much of the development work for the school, sponsoring capital improvements and scholarships.

The school newspapers of the decade make it clear that students had more interaction, beyond the merely social, with other area schools. Lectures and symposia included the participation of other local independent schools. Drama productions and even some religion classes were held in conjunction with The Loyola School.

In 1961-62, new uniforms, with a Campbell tartan kilt and gray blazer, were added to the traditional navy suit.

In the same year, yearbooks were discontinued in all RSHM schools in order to give students a "fuller, richer, education with a positive emphasis on spiritual development." The *Joritan* article states, "At first notice, the motives for this communication . . . were not completely comprehended by the Student Body," but then it goes on to defer to the official explanation. One suspects, however, that alumnae from the classes of 1962 to 1965 still wish they had their yearbooks.

Chapter Seven:
THE SIXTIES
A CHANGING
WORLD

Upper School students supplement their study of geometry via TV, 1960.

Class VIII students at work on Chez Nous, *the Junior School newspaper, 1960*

The June issues of the *Joritan* that contained the graduation photos and write-ups that would have gone into the yearbook could not replace an actual yearbook.

The students were also more vocal about other issues. They objected to local coffee shops charging a minimum so that they could not sit for hours talking while they nursed a coke; and they began to question the practice of freshman initiation. The *Joritan* also recorded the increasing presence of pop culture in student life. Students attended the 1964 World's Fair, and seniors Christina Krupka and Joanne Safian were able

to meet the Beatles, also in 1964. (Christina's father, Henry Krupka of D'Arlene Studios was the official photographer at the Plaza Hotel.) A letter to the editor in a 1960 *Joritan* even asks for more coverage of the new technologies–miniature and compact Princess phones and portable televisions.

Throughout the decade, Marymount's focus on academic excellence never diminished. Students continued their study of the humanities and arts. The introduction of Advanced Placement courses made Marymount an educational leader among schools

Upper School students lay out the Envoy, *the Marymount literary magazine, 1960.*

Le Cercle Français, the French language club, led by Mlle. St. Louis

1960
John F. Kennedy is elected President

1961
East Germany erects the Berlin Wall

Christina Krupka '64 meets The Beatles at the Plaza.

NASA, the American Institute of Physics, and various universities. The symposium earned science teacher Sister Gerard Kern letters of commendation from the White House Science and Technology Department and from NASA.

Marymount's science curriculum was also revised and intensified during the early 1960s. A new P.S.S.C. (Physical Science Study Commission) physics course from Harvard and a new chemistry course, Chemical Educational Material Study ("Chem Study" for short), were introduced. In both courses, the emphasis shifted from factual recall to understanding and applying principles. Laboratory experiments led the student toward discovering rather than proving. This course was highlighted in the Bulletin of the Association of Teachers in Independent Schools of New York. In biology, students

sponsored by religious congregations. Students were also learning Russian and studying the history of communism. In 1963, they were among the first invited to visit the exhibit of the Mona Lisa at The Metropolitan Museum of Art. Special events such as the Shakespeare College Bowl to mark the 400th anniversary of Shakespeare's birth also had an academic focus. In 1966-67, a literature symposium was held to complement the previous science symposium. In 1966, the National Honor Society chartered a *Marifia* Chapter.

At the same time, Marymount's curriculum evolved to keep up with emerging areas of knowledge. With the acceleration of the space race subsequent to the USSR's launching of Sputnik in 1957, Marymount students followed Alan Shepard's first suborbital flight and John Glenn's historic orbiting of the earth. Upper class students were even allowed to attend the ticker-tape parade for Glenn. Between 1962 and 1964, speakers from NASA and various universities addressed the students about the space race. In 1965, Marymount hosted a space symposium, sponsored by the National Science Foundation, for independent school faculty and students. Guest speakers included scientists from

Senior honor students (Class of 1960) with the Scholastic Plaque. The Plaque was the award given to the class that maintained the highest standards of scholastic achievement for the year.

1962

| Vatican II is opened by Pope John XXIII | Cuban Missile Crisis ends with Russians withdrawing missiles | John Glenn orbits the earth | Silent Spring by Rachel Carson describes environmental disasters |

Some members of the Class of '61 after winning the Spirit Cup as Juniors. A coveted honor, the Spirit Cup was given to the class that demonstrated the greatest school spirit. Criteria included: cooperation within the class, cooperation with other classes, respect for rules and regulations, participation in all school events, and respect for authority, student council, and faculty.

Class of 1964 after winning the Basketball Cup

Riding Club in Central Park

1963

200,000 civil rights Freedom Marchers go to Washington	*Martin Luther King, Jr. delivers the "I Have A Dream" speech*

Some members of the Class of 1964 with Senator Barry Goldwater on a senior class visit to Washington, D.C.

the Bay of Pigs crisis, were all subjects for discussion in classes. The tide of conservatism sweeping the country was also felt at Marymount. The Easter edition of the 1962 *Joritan* records that Marymount students attended an Americans for Freedom rally at Madison Square Garden where Barry Goldwater was the featured speaker and in 1964, on a class trip to Washington, D.C., several students met Senator Goldwater. By 1966, the *Joritan* contained the results of a student survey concerning the "Viet Nam Crisis" and the recognition of "Red China" by the United States.

Of course, the major political event of the first half of the decade was the assassination of President John F. Kennedy on Friday, November 22, 1963. At the time of the assassination, Marymount high school students were in the auditorium presenting a feast day program for Reverend Mother Berchmans Walsh. After the program, students were preparing to go home, when Mother Antoine Campbell came out of her office and told the students in the nearby hallways and classrooms what had happened. They crowded into Mother Antoine's office and stood there silently listening to the radio. School was closed as the entire nation observed the official days of mourning and followed both the ceremonies and Jack Ruby's killing of Lee Harvey Oswald on television. The religious community offered Mass for the late president during these

using the new B.S.C.S. (Biological Science Curriculum Study) materials hosted students from the Convent of the Sacred Heart (91st Street) for a lecture on genetics by Dr. H. Burr Rooney from the University of Houston. In fact, science students at Marymount produced a magazine called *Scientific Dimensions*, which contained articles from the biology, physics, and chemistry classes. Copies were distributed to every science student and were also sent to some of the area independent schools.

Politics and world events were also given much attention at Marymount during the 1960s. With the televised Nixon-Kennedy debates, students became much more engaged in the political process. The space race with the USSR, with its political ramifications, as well as the continuation of the Cold War, and especially

1963

John F. Kennedy is assassinated; Lyndon Johnson assumes Presidency   *Betty Friedan's The Feminine Mystique energizes the Women's Movement*

First Formers (freshmen), Class of 1963, having lunch in the dining room

days. When school reopened, the Junior School students participated in a Requiem Mass on November 26 and the high school students did the same on November 27. A condolence card from the entire school was sent to Mrs. Kennedy, who sent a reply.

While science and politics were occupying the minds of the nation, the Second Vatican Council was creating change in the church. Among the most obvious effects of the Council at Marymount was the nuns' adoption of a new habit in January 1963. A short article in the *Joritan* mentions that religious habits are chosen that are "acceptable in a given period, country or class. The costume in the world of 1963 is far removed from that of the French provincial of 1849 when this [Religious of the Sacred Heart of Mary] Institute was founded." This understated acknowledgment of the change does not adequately reflect the hubbub that ensued when the students returned to school after

Christmas vacation and could actually see the nuns' faces more clearly. The chatter and gossip about what the nuns really looked like was the only topic of conversation for several days. The article also ignores the obvious fact that even the new habit looked nothing like the "costume" worn by American women in 1963. It was also during this era that the RSHM changed their form of address from "Mother," "Madame," and "Sister," to one form, "Sister," to emphasize a sense of community and sisterhood rather than maternalism.

The year 1963 also brought the deaths of Pope John XXIII on March 6th and of the RSHM General Superior, Mother Rita Rowley on July 1st.

Obituaries and articles in local newspapers extolled Mother Rita as an educator, noting her advanced degrees from the Sorbonne in Paris, McGill University in Montreal, and Laval University in Quebec. The press cited her work in modernizing the order, in

1965

The first U.S. combat troops arrive in Vietnam

Major demonstrations in Washington against the war in Vietnam

RSHM modified habits in 1963

Members of the class of 1962 at Junior-Senior Tea

Senior chemistry class, 1960

founding schools in Florida, St. Louis, and Chicago; in fostering ministry to the poor in South America; and in raising the number of assistants general from four to six, so that all of the RSHM provinces at that time (France, Brazil, Portugal, England, Ireland, and Eastern and Western North America) would have representation at the Institute level. Mother Rita is buried in the crypt beneath Butler Memorial Chapel in Tarrytown, where Mother Gerard Phelan and Mother Butler are also buried.

Not surprisingly, the years surrounding the Second Vatican Council brought changes in attitudes and new theological approaches to Marymount students. The November 1962 *Joritan* contains articles about the expectations for the Council, and the March 1964 edition recounts the events of an Ecumenical Week held at Marymount. Guest speakers representing the Greek Orthodox, Lutheran, and Jewish faiths addressed the students. In 1967, another symposium and subsequent lectures on ecumenism were held featuring Roman Catholic, Greek Orthodox, and Jewish theologians. Students were educated about other religions, the

Teahouse, Class of 1962

1965

The Beatles' Hard Day's Night tops the music charts

Martin Luther King, Jr. leads civil rights march in Selma, Alabama

ministerial role of the laity, and the concept of Catholics being part of a larger Christian community — all new ideas at the time. Religion class became a place for discussions. Social consciousness and action were more strongly emphasized, and students as well as lay and religious faculty participated in community service programs. Even college choices were affected by the changes in attitudes, as it became more acceptable for students to attend non-Catholic colleges.

The mid-sixties also brought new administrators to Marymount. Sister Marguerite McLoughlin served as superior from 1965 until 1968 and Sister Kevin Tweddle served as principal of the high school during these same years. Sister Christine Marie Mockler and Sister Ann Marie Mooney headed the Junior School during these years.

First Communion, 1965

Junior School students in a music class

*Class of 1962
visiting the
Capitol*

*Class of 1963,
Commencement*

*Class of 1964,
Commencement*

*Class of 1965,
Senior Prom*

*As yearbooks were
not published from
1962-1965,
photos for those
years are shown.*

Students gather on the 1027 staircase in the late 1960s

Y THE last years of the 1960s, the pace of change in the world and in the United States was accelerating, and Marymount was not immune. Traditions that had long been part of the school began to be replaced or reformed. Marymount's system of governance, its curriculum, and its school plant were subject to review.

In 1968 and 1969, *Joritan* articles mention the assassinations of the Reverend Martin Luther King, Jr. and Senator Robert Kennedy, the flight of Apollo 8, the capture of the Pueblo, the deadlock of the Paris negotiations, the failure of Senator Eugene McCarthy to win the Democratic nomination for President, and student participation in a city-wide forum on race relations. It is clear that students were not only well informed about current events but that they also continued to view their own school newspaper as a vehicle to cover more than in-school events. One also remembers that 1969 was the year of Woodstock, of the beginning of the gay-rights movement in New York with the Stonewall rebellion, and the first in-vitro fertilization of a human embryo.

By 1968, the effects of the Second Vatican Council's documents on the church and on religious life were evident among the Religious of the Sacred Heart of Mary and at Marymount School. A major intent of the Council was to view the church from a new perspective. Religious orders were encouraged to integrate themselves more fully into the world. In 1968, the Religious of the Sacred Heart of Mary, convened in General Chapter, offered the sisters the option to wear secular dress, on the principle that religious habits had originally been modeled after the common dress of women of the particular era and country. It was also at this time that many RSHM chose to live outside of the traditional convent structure in smaller groups to emphasize the importance of community. Both the changes in dress and in community living were intended to enable the religious to become more fully inserted

Chapter Eight:
INTO THE SEVENTIES
MAJOR CHANGES
REALIZED

among the people to and with whom they ministered.

Other changes resulting from Vatican II affected attitudes toward lifestyles and ministry. With the affirmation that marriage and single life were lifestyles as Christian and holy as religious life, a number of nuns and priests at this time reassessed their initial choices and left religious life. Many RSHM opted for new ministries that had not been available to them during the years they were semi-cloistered. Thus, they worked in parishes or as campus ministers, social workers, lawyers, and they worked hand in hand with their lay colleagues in their ministries.

One practical consequence of these changes was that religious communities had fewer members available to staff their schools. Additionally, many Catholics of the era were puzzled by the changes in the church, in religious life, and in Catholic schools, and there was some decline in school enrollment as a result. This factor, coupled with the finances needed to support schools staffed by additional lay faculty and fewer sisters, constituted a great challenge for religious communities and their institutions.

At Marymount, the challenges were met, and after a period of transition, the school emerged with a reorganized system of governance and administrative structure.

In 1968-69, under the leadership of Sister Teresita Fay, religious superior and headmistress, the school began the process of incorporating as an entity

Marymount annual School Fair

Sister Genevieve Murphy with Lower School students, 1976

1969
*Apollo astronauts
walk on the moon*

1970
*Four students are slain
at Kent State University*

independent from the religious order. This process began with the recommendation of the Board of Advisors that had been appointed by Sister Teresita Fay, with the approval of Sister Jogues Egan, RSHM, provincial superior. On October 14, 1969, the Board of Regents of the State of New York approved the application for a charter. The corporation's legal existence as Marymount School of New York commenced on that date, which was also the occasion of the first meeting of the new governing entity, a Board of Trustees composed of parents and members of the religious order. The incorporation meant that the legal status of the school now conformed to its reality as an independent institution. Among the advantages of separate incorporation

Marymount's first Board of Trustees as pictured in The Megaphone, *a 1969 school publication. From left: Anthony Peters, Wilmot Mitchell, Sr. Virginia McNally, Sr. Teresita Fay, Sr. Michelle Murphy and Hugo Gerardin*

was that the school would have its own Board of Trustees that would give the school its undivided attention and be fiscally and legally responsible; at the same time, the school would continue its affiliation with the Religious of the Sacred Heart of Mary. The first trustees, Anthony J. Peters, Wilmot B. Mitchell, Hugo J. Gelardin, and RSHM Sisters Michelle Murphy, Virginia McNally, and Teresita Fay, were named by the school's headmistress and the RSHM provincial superior. The Board would shortly be enlarged to include additional lay and religious members.

On the administrative level, there was also ongoing change. In 1968-69, Sister Teresita Fay was assisted by Sister Ann Marie Hill as head of the Upper School and Sister Maureen Vellon as head of the Lower School. In 1969-70, Sister Joan Regis Catherwood became headmistress. While Sister Maureen Vellon continued to lead the Lower School until 1975, Sister Ann Marie Hill was succeeded first by Sister Frances Fisher and then by Brother Thomas Kane, the first non-RSHM

Each year, the senior class decorates the Christmas tree according to Marymount tradition. Tiny white lights and red pears or apples, each bearing the name of a student in the school, are placed on the tree.

1971
26th Amendment to the U.S. Constitution lowers voting age to 18

1972
Gloria Steinem's Ms *magazine debuts*

Students practice on the balance beam, 1974.

Lower School classrroom, 1975

head of a division. By the 1972-73 school year, Sister Catherine Mary Patten became headmistress and Sister Kathleen Fagan head of the Upper School.

Marymount's academic vision remained strong. Under the leadership of Sister Catherine Mary Patten, Sister Kathleen Fagan, and Sister Maureen Vellon, Marymount received accreditation from the Middle States Association. In May 1973, the school was admitted

to the Guild of Independent Schools, and was formally accepted into the New York State Association of Independent Schools.

The school structure itself also evolved. In September 1973, an all-day kindergarten was reinstated. In 1974, the school was reconfigured so that the Lower School encompassed grades Nursery-VI and the Upper School grades VII-XII.

Field Day in Central Park, 1978

1974
*Cultural Revolution
in China begins*

1975
*U.S. Army helicopters
airlift U.S. civilians
from Saigon*

I AM grateful for the education and the opportunities I received from Marymount. I entered the eighth grade in 1974 and graduated in the class of 1979, and my experiences at the school go far beyond the invaluable education that I still look to today.

I was born with cerebral palsy, and legally blind. I have only peripheral, or "outline," vision in one eye and can see very little light out of the other. I have full use of only my right hand and very little use of my left hand and leg. When I began elementary school in 1967, there was no concept of "mainstreaming"— that is, of having children with disabilities learning in the same classroom as their "normal" peers. As a result, for six years I attended a public school and was taught in a classroom with other blind children. I was mainstreamed for the first time in seventh grade.

At the time I entered Marymount, I was the first disabled person ever to be accepted, and in 1979, I was the first disabled person to graduate. I have very fond memories of how the faculty accommodated my unique needs and gave me tools that I value today. I am especially grateful to Sister Melchior Biegen for her patience in the one-on-one tutoring in Algebra I. Mrs. Theresa Bellew introduced me, for the first time, to the study of history, and showed me how to construct an essay. Sister Theresa Fahey taught me how to write, and I attribute my love of writing today to her inspiration. Mr. Ken Zwoloski and Mr. Charles Ippolito administered all the science tests orally. I am also grateful to the students for accepting me as a peer. I read my textbooks on tape and typed my papers with one hand. I realize this was probably the first time the faculty and students were exposed to working and learning with someone with a disability. I am indebted to everyone I met at Marymount for their support and sensitivity, and for treating me like everyone else.

I currently work for Community Access, a nonprofit organization in New York City. Community Access has housing, vocational, and advocacy programs for adults with psychiatric disabilities. For five years, I worked for Community Access's transitional housing program, which helps adults who have been homeless or in psychiatric hospitals. I counseled, advocated, and escorted clients to appointments. Now I am training, counseling, and advocating for people with psychiatric disabilities to work with others with such disabilities. The tools I learned at Marymount continue to serve me well.

By JUSTINE HOPPER, Class of '79

In order to accommodate the continued growth of the school and to utilize space more effectively, a renovation was undertaken during the summer of 1969. JFN Associates and contractor H. L. Lazar donated their services to the school. Walls were erected in order to create small rooms for student-teacher conferences and the 1027 parlor was partitioned into three offices for administrators and secretaries. The chapel was subdivided to become two classrooms and a smaller chapel; the entrance hall of 1026 was redesigned to create an admissions office, and the second floor landings of 1026 and 1027 were also subdivided. Most of the partitions have since been removed in order to restore the original elegant spaces.

In the early 1970s, the parents' groups were also reorganized. According to the minutes of the Board of Trustees, a Parents' Association was formed. The Parents' Association is listed as the host for the 1969 Spring Dinner Dance, and it has hosted this event, a major fundraising endeavor now known as the Spring Benefit Gala, ever since.

While the school's Alumnae Association met occasionally during the 1960s, in January 1970, it was

50th Anniversary Jubilee flag, 1976

Dinner Dance invitation, 1971

reorganized on a more formal basis. A letter that year from Alumnae Association President Cornelia Ladas Bauer Iredell '55 articulates the need for a renewed connection between the school and its alumnae. In 1972, twelve alumnae officers and class agents met with Sister Joan Regis Catherwood and Sister Antoine Campbell to revitalize the association. In September 1975, the president of the Alumnae Association became an *ex officio* member of the Board of Trustees, as did the president of the Parents' Association. During this time, alumnae became involved as speakers for senior seminars and as sponsors for senior internships, bringing together students and alumnae from various professions and planting the seeds of "networking."

1975
*The Vietnam War
ends*

1976
*American Bicentennial
is celebrated*

Jubilee Mass at the Church of St. Ignatius Loyola, Terence Cardinal Cooke celebrating.

By the 1976-77 school year, many of the transitions had been accomplished. Sister Kathleen Fagan, head of the Upper School, became headmistress. She was assisted by a dean of studies, Sister Dorothy Donovan, and a dean of students, Sister Theresa Fahey. Sister Jacquelyn Porter became head of the Lower School and director of admissions. In 1979, Sister Clevie Youngblood became head of the Upper School.

The role of the Board of Trustees also expanded. A Development Committee of the Board oversaw all fundraising activities, and the first director of development, Valery Shields Shea '59, was appointed. The first annual fund drive was begun in 1973.

In February 1976, Marymount celebrated its 50th anniversary. A Jubilee Mass was celebrated by Terence Cardinal Cook at the Church of St. Ignatius Loyola, and a gala celebration was held at The Metropolitan Museum of Art. Jubilee week at school was commemorated with special workshop days and learning activities in both the Upper and Lower Schools.

Academic developments during the latter years of the decade included the institution of a community service program in the high school and the offering of high school math, science, and language courses to qualified eighth-grade students. The senior internship program gained momentum, and computer-assisted instruction first came to Marymount as early as 1978.

Clearly, Marymount students continued to be very much in touch with current issues and intent on voicing their own opinions, questioning the status quo, and making proposals. Student publications of these years contain letters requesting more electives and more student representation concerning administrative matters. For example, there are discussions about social issues, support for the United Farm Workers' boycott of

Terence Cardinal Cooke and Sister Catherine Mary Patten greeting guests after the Jubilee Mass. Student Kathy Mitchell is shown at right.

1977
Rosalyn Yalow wins Nobel Prize in Medicine

1978
For the first time, more women than men enter college

grapes and iceberg lettuce, and the role of women. A 1978 letter to the editor of the *Joritan* asserts that the students' goals are no longer "to destroy the establishment, but rather to attain the highest position possible within it. The efforts of the women's movement have also added incentive to today's high school girls to move upward."

In 1977, the Landmarks Preservation Commission designated the Metropolitan Museum Historic District. This meant that all buildings within the district boundaries were under special protection and

Lower School students at music class

that no modifications to buildings could be made without the permission of the Landmarks Preservation Commission. Sister Kathleen Fagan mentioned the acquiring of landmark status in her 1977 Annual Report, saying that "it rooted Marymount more deeply than ever in the neighborhood and will, hopefully, provide new means of outreach to the community."

Lower School uniforms, 1970s

In the early 1970s, uniforms became optional in the Upper School. Most students chose not to wear them. Required uniforms returned in the late 1970s. Lower School students continued to wear a one-piece dress.

Upper School uniforms in the late 1970s-early 80s

1978
*John Paul II
becomes Pope*

1979
*Mother Teresa of Calcutta
wins Nobel Peace Prize*

Sister Kathleen Fagan, RSHM

Sister Kathleen Fagan, a native of New York City, attended Marymount School from 1955 to 1959. She entered the Religious of the Sacred Heart of Mary in Tarrytown in 1959 and earned her Bachelor's degree from Marymount College, Tarrytown.

Sister Kathleen taught at Marymount International School in Surrey, England, from 1963 until 1965 and at the RSHM school in Sag Harbor, New York, from 1965 to 1968. She earned her Master's degree from the University of Notre Dame in 1969 and returned that year to Marymount School Fifth Avenue as chair of the English Department. She became divisional head of the Upper School in 1972 and headmistress in 1976.

The Board of Trustees, on the occasion of the celebration of Sr. Kathleen's twenty-fifth anniversary as Headmistress of Marymount School, presented her with an encomium . . .

"A superb spokesperson for the School and a consummate leader, Kathleen's innovation, diligence, oversight and determination have placed Marymount among the top independent schools dedicated to the education of young women. Her commitment to academic excellence is reflected in the School's outstanding curriculum, wide range of service projects and numerous extracurricular offerings. Her dedication and attention to detail have been crucial in guiding the School through years of growth and expansion, bringing the School to financial stability and implementing long-range improvements, including a new gymnasium, new science and technology facilities, and, most recently, a new building for the Middle School.

"While attending to her responsibilities at Marymount she has generously shared her wisdom and expertise, serving on the Boards of numerous schools , colleges and educational organizations.

"It is with tremendous gratitude and affection that we offer our thanks for Kathleen's dedicated stewardship, genuine love of Marymount and unstinting service to our community. Through her guidance, Marymount continues to fulfil the vision of Mother Butler and the RSHM as we enter a bright new century. Her own high standards, sense of fairness and deeply rooted spiritual values serve as a model for students and faculty, who are encouraged and challenged on a daily basis to 'question, risk and grow.'"

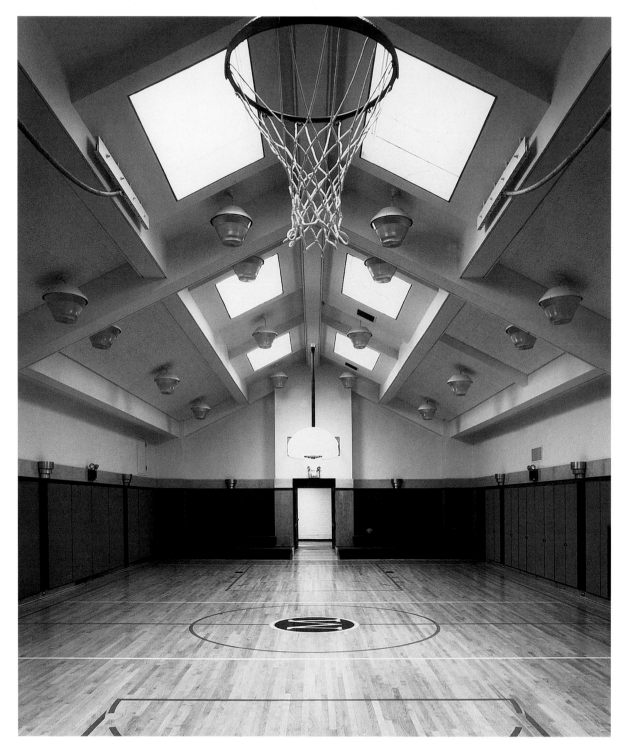

The new gymnasium, 1984

BY 1979, the Board of Trustees commenced a planning study for the better utilization of space in the buildings. It was apparent that the continued growth in the educational program required improved facilities. Two areas in particular—the science laboratories and physical education facilities—were identified. In 1979, the firm of Buttrick, White & Burtis produced the first architectural survey of the three mansion buildings. A major undertaking of the early 1980s was the planning and construction of a new gymnasium.

At this time, Marymount launched its first capital campaign. Pat Barter, past parent and former president of the Parents' Association, was hired to be its director. With a plan to raise $1.3 million, the first phase goal was to fund the rooftop gymnasium and provide monies for special operating support over the three years of the capital campaign. With the support of the Board of Trustees, a group of enthusiastic parents, alumnae, and staff began fundraising for the project. With 60% of the funds raised, a reception and dinner was held at the Plaza Hotel on October 20, 1981, to announce the public phase. Over 335 alumnae, parents, and friends attended to celebrate the campaign. As David Hume, Headmaster of Saint David's School and a trustee of Marymount, pointed out in his keynote address: "Marymount has done a remarkable thing. In the last five years, the school has grown almost half again as large. Marymount's place in the shifting educational sociology of New York is a new and stronger one than ever before." Three RSHM, Sisters Genevieve Toner, Elizabeth Gallagher, and Antoine Campbell, were honored at the reception. These women had collectively served the Marymount students and families for almost 90 years.

Chapter Nine:
THE EIGHTIES EXPANSION AND NEW PROJECTS

Sisters Elizabeth Gallagher, Genevieve Toner, and Antoine Campbell honored at the Plaza Hotel, 1981

curriculum was introduced in 1985, and interscholastic competition in team sports dramatically expanded.

The 1980s also saw continued restructuring in organization and administration. When Sister Clevie Youngblood left for Marymount Rome, the Upper School was led by Sister Mary McHugh in 1985 and then by Mrs. Irene McCreery in 1988. In the Lower School, Sister Jacquelyn Porter was succeeded by Sister Nancy Callahan, SHCJ (Sisters of the Holy Child of Jesus) in 1981 and then by Joyce Dupee in 1983. Mrs. Dupee was the first divisional head at Marymount who was not a religious.

In addition to fundraising, zoning was another major hurdle before the gymnasium could be constructed. Because Marymount is located in an historic district, approval from the Landmarks Preservation Commission was needed in order to change the exterior of the building. Eventually this was accomplished, and construction began during the summer of 1983. However, construction stopped at the beginning of the school year because tenants of neighboring buildings, fearful that the addition would obstruct their view of Central Park, sued to halt work and were granted an injunction. The petition was short-lived, and by late fall the project was again on course.

Even though construction and bad weather resulted in leaky ceilings, plastic drapes, umbrellas indoors, and frequently relocated classes, progress continued through the winter and into spring. The gymnasium was officially opened on May 31, 1984, to great fanfare.

With this addition, physical education classes and home athletic events no longer had to be held at The Loyola School, the 92nd Street Y, or other gyms. With the new facility, a revised physical education

A science class, c. 1981

1981

Ronald Reagan is inaugurated

52 American hostages freed by Iran

In 1989, Marymount's Middle School division, classes IV through VII, was created to address the specific needs of pre-adolescent girls. With one class per grade level and classes situated in the same area (the fifth floor of the 1026 and 1027 buildings), teachers who were experts in Middle School curriculum and pedagogy established a strong program. Mrs. Lillian Issa, a former fifth grade teacher, provided leadership as the first Middle School head. A hallmark of the program was an interdisciplinary curriculum focusing on collaborative projects and study and research skills. After-school sports, clubs, an annual drama performance, and overnight trips also became mainstays of the Middle School program.

Construction of the new gymnasium

With the completion of the new gym, it was also possible to hold gatherings for the entire school in this space.

Construction of the new gymnasium on the roof

1981
Sandra Day O'Connor becomes first woman on U.S. Supreme Court

1982
Equal Rights Amendment fails to win ratification in the House of Representatives

The Basketball Story

MARYMOUNT has not always been a basketball power. Anyone associated with the school's athletic program in 1986 would have laughed at the suggestion that the "Lions" would soon become league champions, and in subsequent years a juggernaut attracting city-wide recognition.

The players who came to tryouts in my first season as coach were an eager but inexperienced group. Since some could not make a basket from the regulation foul line, I used tape to create a closer line that helped our beginners develop confidence while learning proper technique. That first group of students was unfailingly kind, so that when one fell down during a scrimmage, everyone on both teams stopped to make sure she was all right. The ethic was admirable, but it would not lead to victories, so I went to talk with the headmistress. While I was prepared to coach a polite and courteous team that might win an occasional game, I also suggested we could find a way to become more aggressive and competitive. Eager to instill tenacity and confidence, Sister Kathleen gave her approval.

That conversation signaled a turning point in the basketball program. The ascent had begun. The team grew stronger through the addition of athletes who brought a combination of physical talent and psychological toughness. The '92-'93 team won both the regular season title and the post-season tournament as the perennial also-rans had become champions. And the tape that had once marked makeshift foul lines now found a better use—holding up the banners.

By ROBERT MULGREW, English Department and Coach
(1986-1993)

WHEN I arrived at Marymount for the '93-'94 season, I inherited the same team that had won the previous year's AAIS Championship—minus one: a star player. My top priority was to convince the returning players that they were still good enough to win. We struggled early, learned to trust one another, and finished strong in the AAIS Finals.

In the '94-'95 season, four fabulous freshmen joined our program and provided the commitment to excellence that made us a very talented team. With the seniors providing the leadership and the freshmen the enthusiasm, we fulfilled our destiny and won the state championship. Marymount had its own "Dream Team." The Lions were a team of outstanding young women who worked tirelessly, believed and trusted in one another, and discovered that "dreams do come true."

In the seasons from 1993 to the present, Marymount Varsity Basketball teams have accomplished:

7 AAIS Tournament Championships
'93, '95, '96, '97, '98, '00, '01
3 AAIS regular season Championships '92-'93, '94-'95, '97-'98
1 NYSAIS Championship '95
1 undefeated season '94-'95

During my tenure at Marymount, I have been lucky enough to coach some very successful teams, but I am most proud of the sense of intelligence and humanity displayed by the young women who have given their all for the sake of their teammates. Through their dedication, sacrifice, and tenacity, they have made the "Lions" the team that it is today.

By MATT YOUNG (One Very Happy Coach)

1993 AAIS Championship Basketball Team

1995 AAIS Basketball Champions

Today's Sports

While the athletic program during Marymount's first decades concentrated on basketball and field hockey, students at Marymount today are given the option of competing in a wide variety of sports. In addition to basketball, Marymount fields the following teams:

Field Hockey

Badminton

Volleyball

Tennis

Softball

Track & Field

Swimming

Fencing

Soccer

Cross Country

Golf

Lower School Art

Upper School Studio Art, Art Department Chair
Barbara Ledig-Sheehan, on right.

Shakespeare Festival competition, 1980s

Middle School students participating in the Advent Festival
of Lessons and Carols, a celebration of the Christmas story.

1983
Sally Ride, first
woman in space, on
the crew of the
Challenger

1984
Apple introduces the
Macintosh computer

Sixtieth Anniversary of Marymount School 1986

Marymount celebrates its 60th Anniversary with a Mass on Founder's Day at the Church of St. Ignatius Loyola, on February 2, 1986.
Father Edward M. Egan was the celebrant of the Mass and David Dinkins, Manhattan Borough President, declared February 2, 1986 "Marymount Day."
Edward A. Koch, Mayor of New York City, joined the community for the birthday party at the school
and became an "Honorary Marymounter."

Mayor Ed Koch joins in the celebration of the 60th Jubilee

Student Government members applaud as Manhattan Borough President
David Dinkins proclaims February 2, 1986 "Marymount Day."

1984
Geraldine Ferraro is the
first woman candidate
for Vice-President chosen
by a major political party

1985
British scientists discover
hole in the ozone layer

Seniors lead an after-school
CCD (Confraternity of Christian Doctrine) Class.

Class II, First Communion, 1987

The first Marymount skating parties took place at Rockefeller Center.
The event was later moved to Wollman Memorial Rink in Central Park.

1986
Space shuttle
Challenger explodes
on launch

1987
Dow Jones falls 508 points on
October 19, after record high
of 2722.42

Senior retreat at Cormaria, Sag Harbor, New York, 1986

In 1985, a summer program was started for children ages three to eight. The goal was to provide a well-structured, intellectually stimulating program that would also be fun. Thirty-four children attended in the program's first year. By 1989, 100 children joined and in the summer of 2000, 375 children participated in three programs. A Drama Camp was added in 1990, and a Science and Technology program for children ages nine to twelve was started in 1995. Marymount Summer admits both boys and girls and employs many Marymount Upper School students as counselors.

Science labs under construction–Sister Kathleen with Middle School students, 1994

BY THE 1990s, further attention was given to the expansion and enhancement of specific programs, as well as to the growth of the entire school. A healthy economic climate, the rise of interest in single-sex education, and Marymount's own quality programs all led to a significant increase in enrollment.

Having rebuilt its athletic facilities in the 1980s, Marymount continued to develop its sports programs, and Marymount teams were winning titles in several sports, including basketball, track and field, and swimming.

On an entirely different note, the past twenty years have also seen Marymount's heightened commitment to diversity. In the late 1980s, in conjunction with workshops conducted by the New York State Association of Independent Schools, Marymount initiated a Multicultural Committee. In February 1991, an African-American Book Fair, coordinated by parent Jeanne Moutoussamy-Ashe, was held. Mrs. Joyce B. Dinkins made the opening remarks, and Arthur Ashe and Bryant Gumbel, also Marymount parents, were among those who read to the students. Storyteller Rette DeVille, writer Elizabeth Alexander, anchorwoman Lynne White, illustrators Brian Pinckney and Floyd Cooper, and Mets left fielder George Foster all participated. In subsequent years, programs such as "Roots and Branches," the Jazz Concert, and Harambee were developed. The Multicultural Club, which evolved into the Cultural Awareness Club, was a student discussion group comprised of students of many nationalities and ethnicities.

Marymount also expanded the boundaries of its community through a cultural exchange and immersion program that began in 1999 and continues. Marymount students have enjoyed exchange experiences with Native American students from the Santa Fe Indian School in Santa Fe, New Mexico, and have also

Chapter Ten:
THE NINETIES
INTO THE NEW
MILLENNIUM

Arthur Ashe, with daughter Camera, reading to students as part of the African-American Book Fair.

Joyce Dinkins, First Lady of the City of New York, visits the Book Fair.

had the opportunity to travel and study for several weeks in Japan and China, experiences that afforded intense immersion in these cultures. Students from these areas have also spent up to three weeks at Marymount.

In the 1990s, Marymount began the second phase of its original capital campaign. In 1992, the school embarked on the "Campaign for Science" to finance the construction of three new science labs that were to be relocated to the upper floors of the 1026 and 1027 buildings. Pat Barter again became the campaign director. In 1994, a "Year of Science" was launched with a science symposium on Founder's Day, February 2nd. Student presentations and experiments, panels and seminars, and a keynote address by Dr. Rosalyn Yalow, a 1977 Nobel Prize winner for Medicine, highlighted the day. The new state-of-the-art science center was ready

Harambee–a Swahili word meaning "to unite in celebration"–is hosted every February by the Cultural Awareness Club.

1990

East and West Germany reunite after 45-year division

Iron Curtain countries rebel against Communist form of government

Iraq invades Kuwait

Science Symposium

Science Symposium program

As part of the Campaign for Science, a special Founder's Day Science Symposium was held on February 2, 1994.

The entire Marymount community celebrated by participating in science experiments, presentations, and discussions on scientific ethics. The highlight of the day was the address given by Dr. Rosalyn Yalow, 1977 Nobel Prize winner for Medicine.

Dr. Rosalyn Yalow (right), with Dr. Jane Haher-Izquierdo '58 (center), at the Science Symposium.

A parent assists her daughter with a science experiment during the Science Symposium.

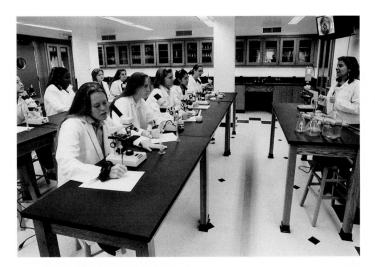

An Upper School biology class in the Life Science Lab, 1994

for September 1994, and on October 4th, more than 500 alumnae, parents, past parents and friends gathered to view it and to see students demonstrate the technology and equipment. While computer-assisted instruction and a computer programming elective in the Upper School had begun at Marymount in 1978, technology gained momentum with the installation of a network as part of the new science labs and the establishment of a new technology center. A technology plan was developed with major goals being the wiring of the entire school for a computer network, additional computer stations, high-speed Internet access, and e-mail accounts for Upper School students and staff. The Marymount Web site opened in 1996 and served as a portal for Internet access and a showcase of student work. Collaborative education took hold as students created e-businesses with students at Marymount High School in Los Angeles and Marymount International School in Rome and communicated with scientists living in Antarctica. PBS Channel 13 and BBC Worldwide radio have showcased Marymount's technology programs.

During the 1990s, Marymount continued to benefit from the leadership of a number of able administrators. The Upper School was administered by the effective leadership of Irene McCreery and, more recently, Carole France. During the 1990s, Susan Johnson and Beth Sullivan led the Lower and Middle Schools, strengthening curriculum and providing a strong foundation for others to follow.

In 1998, however, Marymount lost one of its most beloved educators. Sister Antoine Campbell first came to Marymount in 1929 as a Latin and history teacher and remained until 1936. In 1953, she returned to Marymount and served as head of the Upper School until 1966. She also taught speech and Latin. She returned again to Marymount as Latin teacher and alumnae director from 1968 to 1991, the year she retired. For many alumnae, memories of Marymount are inextricably intertwined with memories of Sister Antoine's recitations of *The Aeneid*, checking that tams and gloves were in place, practicing proper pronunciation when in her presence, imitating her distinctive voice when she was out of earshot, and discovering her sparkling wit when one was old enough to appreciate it.

In the 1990s, the Alumnae Association also began some new initiatives aimed especially at inviting alumnae to return to school and become more involved. Trips to the New York Botanical Garden and to museums, lectures on various topics, and regional events in Boston, Washington, D.C., and Florida have all fostered networking and alumnae support for the school.

Skating Party at Wollman Memorial Rink in Central Park

1990
Nelson Mandela
freed from prison

1991
U.S., backed by UN, begins war with Iraq and defeats Saddam Hussein's troops

1992
William Jefferson Clinton is elected President

Sisters Lucille Melo, Paulina Ferrao, and Scholastica Gonzalez. These beloved Sisters, seen here at a Faculty-Trustee Christmas party, retired from Marymount School in 1999. Sister Paulina had served thirty-four years at Marymount, Sister Lucille thirty-three years, and Sister Scholastica thirty years.

Carolyn Booth, Spiritual Life Director (right), and students at an Upper School chapel service

Lower School Christmas Pageant

The 150th Anniversary of the Religious of the Sacred Heart of Mary

In 1999, the Religious of the Sacred Heart of Mary celebrated the 150th anniversary of their founding with a Mass at St. Patrick's Cathedral. Marymount students, teachers, parents, and alumnae were invited to join the RSHM on this special occasion.

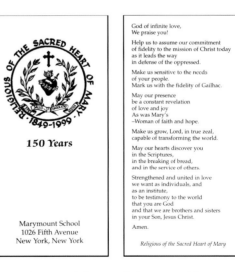

RELIGIOUS OF THE SACRED HEART OF MARY
1849-1999

150 Years

Marymount School
1026 Fifth Avenue
New York, New York

God of infinite love,
We praise you!

Help us to assume our commitment
of fidelity to the mission of Christ today
as it leads the way
in defense of the oppressed.

Make us sensitive to the needs
of your people.
Mark us with the fidelity of Gailhac.

May our presence
be a constant revelation
of love and joy
As was Mary's
–Woman of faith and hope.

Make us grow, Lord, in true zeal,
capable of transforming the world.

May our hearts discover you
in the Scriptures,
in the breaking of bread,
and in the service of others.

Strengthened and united in love
we want as individuals, and
as an institute,
to be testimony to the world
that you are God
and that we are brothers and sisters
in your Son, Jesus Christ.

Amen.

Religious of the Sacred Heart of Mary

Prayer card from 150th Anniversary Mass

*Field Day—a tradition that is a part of
the beginning of each school year*

*Frost Valley. This trip takes place in the first weeks
of each school year. Class IX students go to Frost Valley in upstate
New York to participate in a variety of activities, indoors and out,
that enable them to get to know their classmates and return ready to
start their first year of high school as a unified class.*

Class III students visit The Metropolitan Museum of Art.

Students and faculty participate in New York Cares Day, 1990.

*Father-Daughter Square Dance—a Marymount tradition
in the Middle School*

2001
*On September 11th a
terrorist attack destroys the
World Trade Center buildings
in New York City*

2000
*George W. Bush is
elected President*

The Vincent A. Lisanti Speaker Series

Established in 1996 by alumna and trustee Mary Lisanti '74 in honor of her father, the Vincent A. Lisanti Speaker Series has brought notable writers and thinkers to Marymount. They include the following:

Poets

Billy Collins	United States Poet Laureate
Stephen Dunn	Poet
Joy Harjo	Native American Poet
George Heard	Poet, Columbia University Professor
Naomi Shihab Nye	Palestinian-American Poet
Molly Peacock	Poet, Co-founder of Poetry in Motion
Miller Williams	Inaugural Poet, Clinton Administration

Writers/Playwrights

Linda Fairstein	NYC Assistant District Attorney, Novelist, Feminist
Patricia Hampl	Memoirist
David Huddle	Fiction Writer/Essayist
Alice McDermott	National Book Award-winning Author
Katherine Paterson	Children's Book Author
Mary Rodgers	Playwright

Others

Esther Dyson	Technology Analyst, Futurist
Ronald Green, Ph.D.	Scientist, Dartmouth Professor, NIH Ethicist
Kathy Kater	Speaker, expert on pre-adolescent girls
Nancy Lublin	Founder, Dress for Success
Andrea Marcovicci '66	Singer, Actress
Sarah Spencer	Women's Commission on Refugee Women & Children
Gloria Steinem	Feminist Activist, Author
Helen Thomas	Dean of White House Press Corps
Patricia Williams	MacArthur Fellow, Professor, Lawyer, Author, social justice activist

Speakers heard at the 92nd Street Y:

Seamus Heaney
Alice Walker
Toni Morrison
Arthur Miller
Frank McCourt

Patricia Hampl

Alice McDermott

Ronald Green, Ph.D.

*Patricia Hampl,
Alice McDermott,
and Dr. Ronald Green
spoke during the
75th Anniversary Year.*

Gloria Steinem, 1997

Andrea Marcovicci '66, 1996

Computer Technology

Dorian Deglin, '82 at the mainframe computer workstation

MARYMOUNT'S technology era began in the fall of 1978, with the leasing of three computer terminals that were connected by telephone line to a mainframe computer housed at the Spence Computer Center. Marymount was one of only nine independent schools to participate in this early time-sharing initiative.

The appearance of the three bulky terminals was strikingly different from the computers of today. There were no monitors attached to them; students and faculty had to analyze data from printouts on tractor-feed paper. The new machines intrigued faculty and students alike. Sr. Dorothy Donovan, RSHM, chair of the math department, wrote in the Marymount Newsletter of the terminals' ability to enrich the curriculum by giving students more learning options. 1979 graduate Angelica Ortiz spoke of the potential of the machine to revolutionize the world: "It's such an amazing piece of machinery. There's so much you can do with it—and so much yet to be discovered." Ms. Ortiz went on to study computer engineering at Columbia University's School of Engineering.

Classes in programming languages such as Pascal became a part of the school program during the 1978-1979 school year, and a Computer Programmers Club

was pictured in the 1979 *Marifia*. Students were soon creating programs to record and tabulate the results of student government elections and to identify the binary code for personal names. They even discovered that they could play games of Hangman against the terminals.

In the early 1980s, a collection of Apple II's and IIe's was added, and computers became a greater part of the lives of students. *Marifia* and *Joritan* staff members began to use the Apples as word processors and the publications of that period reflect just how much the editors enjoyed printing titles in new font styles—despite the limitations of dot-matrix printers. The 1981 *Marifia* even punned that the students were in a state of "Terminal Happiness" over the new technology.

The library was also undergoing a computer revolution. Marymount was one of the first independent schools to replace its library's card catalog with a computer database, and the school participated in an inter-library loan initiative by adding its records to a citywide union catalog. Kathy Harshberger, head librarian at the time, was in charge of this time-consuming initiative.

Unlike other institutions, Marymount never went through a "Mac Classic" phase of development but jumped directly from the Apple II's to the Macintosh Power Book. Science department chair Don Buckley made twenty Power Books a part of the 1993-1994 Campaign for Science. These were networked to a file server, making this the first network in the school. The World Wide Web, still in its infancy, was accessible through a very small collection of modems, three of which were utilized by the science department. The modem housed in the library accessed the school's early AOL account and received E-mail messages from the school's first E-mail address: mschool689@aol.com.

After the success of the science department's network, it was decided that the rest of the school should be networked. A faculty committee was created to steer the implementation of new technology. This group wrote a five-year plan that included the wiring and networking of the entire school, laying of a high-speed T-1 line to connect the school to the electronic world, creation of E-mail accounts for all staff and Upper School students, and the development of a Web presence. This ambitious five-year plan was accomplished a year early and established the school as a leader in technology.

More recently, the school has been one of the first independent schools to experiment with wireless technology. In the year 2000, Marymount's technology was recognized by *Our Town* magazine as the best of the private schools on the East Side of Manhattan.

CHRISTMASTIDE compact disc. Marymount Singers recorded live in concert, December 3, 1998.

Students using first laptops, c. 1994, with Don Buckley Science Department Chair

1999 Yearbook on compact disc

The 75th Anniversary Year of Marymount School

MARYMOUNT'S 75th Anniversary was a year of cele-bration and thanksgiving, a year in which alumnae, parents, students, faculty, and friends came together to honor the vision of Mother Butler and the Religious of the Sacred Heart of Mary. It was a year in which the value of "gratitude" was chosen to express the Marymount community's thanks for the blessings of seventy-five extraordi-nary years.

The School's curriculum was showcased as different disciplines were highlighted each month. In honor of January's focus on athletics, Mary-mount's first annual Homecoming took place on the weekend of January 12-13. Basketball games with parents and trustees vs. faculty and with student varsity vs. alumnae varsity were enthu-siastically attended (the parent-trustee and current varsity teams were victori-ous). Following the games, "Trailblaz-ers," student athletes selected from classes 1980 (the year the new gym construction began) through 1994 were inducted onto the "Wall of Fame."

Founder's Day, February 2, 2001, began with trumpets sounding and a cheer as traffic on Fifth Avenue came to a halt. Students, faculty, and adminis-trators assembled on the Avenue to watch as Headmistress, Sister Kathleen Fagan raised Marymount's 75th Anni-versary flag. Carrying red, white, and blue balloons, everyone applauded as the flag waved from the second-floor balcony.

The flag-raising and Founder's Day festivities were followed on February 4th by a Mass of Thanksgiving at the Church of St. Ignatius Loyola. More than one thou-sand parents, faculty, students, alumnae, trustees and friends gathered together as principal celebrant Bishop James F. McCarthy, D.D. addressed the congregation. Students took an active role as banner bearers, lectors, and leaders of song. An adult choir of faculty and friends joined the student choristers as the church was filled

75th Anniversary Mass of Thanksgiving, Church of St. Ignatius Loyola February 4, 2001

with music. Receptions followed at the school and in Wallace Hall at St. Ignatius Loyola.

Later in February, an alumnae regional event was held and videos of the flag-raising and liturgy were shared with members of the Marymount community in Florida. Alumnae from the United States, Canada, Europe, and South America gathered in record num-bers on April 27-29, when the first three-day All-Alumnae Reunion was held. The highlight of the weekend was the 75th Anniversary Spring Benefit Gala, co-hosted by the Parents' and Alumnae Associations at the Plaza Hotel. The evening included a cocktail reception, dinner and dancing, live and silent auctions, a raffle, a commemo-rative journal, and a video tribute.

On June 4th, cabaret came to Mary-mount when Andrea Marcovicci '66 per-formed at a special benefit concert for the school.

In August, the Suskind family hosted Marymount Family Day on the opening day of The Hampton Classic in Bridgehampton, New York. On November 17th, the Marymount Alumnae Associa-tion and the 75th Anniversary Liturgical Committee hosted a "Day of Reflection," led by Mary C. Boys, SNJM. December's holiday events included a screening of the movie, *A Beautiful Mind*, a film directed by a Marymount parent, Ron Howard about the life of John Nash, mathematician, win-ner of the 1994 Nobel Prize in Economic Science, and his wife alumna Alicia Larde Nash '51. The Marymount community joined together for the traditional Lessons and Carols, and the Alumnae and Parents' Associations hosted an evening with Jock Elliot, renowned collector, speaking on "Traditions of Christmas."

The 75th Anniversary year also included archival dis-plays and the 75th Anniversary Lisanti Speaker Series, fea-turing writer Alice McDermott, scientist and ethicist Ron Green, Ph.D., and, memoirist, Patricia Hampl.

The year closed with a Mass of Thanksgiving at the Church of Saint Ignatius Loyola on February 1, 2002.

*Bishop Patrick V. Ahern, D.D., Laudine Vallarta '01,
and Bishop James F. McCarthy, D.D.*

*Sister Elizabeth Gallagher, RSHM (right),
and Sister Letizia Pappalardo RSHM, Provincial,
Eastern American Province*

Class banners lead the procession, February 4, 2001

*"We are filled with gratitude
for the vision of Mother Joseph Butler,
who articulated the mission that continues
to inspire and guide our community, and for
the many Religious whose leadership and
dedication are reflected in the lives of
Marymount alumnae and students. . . .
To Sister Elizabeth and the Religious
of the Sacred Heart of Mary
we offer our deepest thanks.
May they be blessed as they have blessed
all whose lives they have touched."*

*From the encomium presented to
Sister Elizabeth Gallagher and
Sister Letizia Pappalardo*

"Roary the Lion," Marymount's mascot, at the first Homecoming celebration, January 2001

Big and little sisters celebrate Founder's Day, 2001.

Students celebrate their triumph at the TriState Chess Tournament, 2001.

Founder's Day, February 2, 2001

Marymount Rome students join Class VIII's Model Congress during a week-long visit to Marymount New York, 2001.

The Muse, the school's award-winning literary magazine

Juniors on Ring Day, May 2001

Grandparents' and Special Friends' Day is an opportunity for students to share their school with special people, May 2001.

Dr. Jane Haher-Izquierdo '58, President of the Board of Trustees, with 75th Anniversary Honorary Gala Chair, Noriko Maeda

Alumnae Chair Susan Brown Roschen '53, with Parent Chair, Geraldine Jordan

Peter and Erika Aron with Sister Kathleen Fagan and Dr. Jane Haher-Izquierdo '58

Terrace Party Chair Michelle Cox Garcia '89 (center), with husband, Jose Garcia and Susana Acosta

Andrea Marcovicci '66 with the Chairs of the Marcovicci benefit, Kristen Thompson, Jimmie Ritchie, and Joanne Czechlewski Wallace '63

ANDREA MARCOVICCI

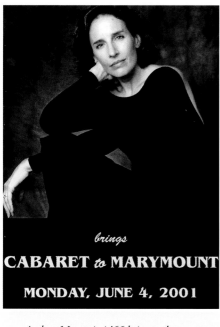

brings
CABARET to MARYMOUNT
MONDAY, JUNE 4, 2001

Andrea Marcovicci '66 brings cabaret to Marymount, June 4, 2001.

Sister Colette McManus (right), with Kathleen Birkey, Head Librarian, Reunion 2001

SISTER COLETTE McMANUS, a native of Dublin, Ireland, taught English and Latin at Marymount from 1946 to 1961. In her fifteen years at the school, she served as an English department chair and the homeroom teacher for junior and senior classes. Sister Colette was one of the teachers who introduced Advanced Placement classes to Marymount and instilled in her students an appreciation for Shakespeare. Marymount was Sister Colette's first teaching assignment and one that she remembers with great fondness. She calls the school her "first love."

After leaving Marymount Fifth Avenue, Sister Colette went on to teach at RSHM schools in Bogota, Colombia, Barcelona, Spain, and Neuilly, France. On her return, she was asked to become an interim head of the RSHM school in Westwood, California, for one year. She stayed for eighteen years.

Today, Sister Colette is a member of the RSHM community in Los Angeles, California. She was honored at Reunion 1999 and joined alumnae again for the 2000 and 2001 reunions.

Marymount Family Day at the Hampton Classic, 2001

Hosts Cynthia and Dennis Suskind

Chairs Jayne Gillette and Gayil Nalls with their daughter

Maryellen McGoldrick Schwarz '56
Regional Events Chair (far left), with Marymount friends

Sister Kathleen Fagan and alumna Holly Aron

ANNIVERSARY

CELEBRATING 75 YEARS OF MARYMOUNT SCHOOL, NEW YORK CITY, 1926-2001

Remembering gathers the years around us,
draws us back to a center that holds us in her grace.
It is in reunion that we recollect.
It is in remembering that we re-belong.

We remember with intention and celebration
all the lives who imagined this place into being
and those who have blessed the unfolding
and folding of each bright year.

We honor this place where girls and young women
learn to imagine what can be,
learn to travel to places beyond the self,
learn to speak with clarity and authority—
learn they may become what they will.

And so we take the past to heart, firmly grounded,
as we dream the future into flesh,
remembering with prayerful thanksgiving
this place, this Marymount School—
diverse, celebratory, rigorous, imperfect, blessed,
Alive!

—CATHY BLACKBURN

(Mrs. Blackburn was Marymount School's Writer-in-Residence and a member of the English department faculty, 1995-2000)

Nobel laureate John Nash, Biographer Silvia Nasar, and Alicia Larde Nash '51 with Sister Kathleen Fagan at a special screening of A Beautiful Mind. *The film is based on the life of Nobel Prize Winner for Economic Science, John Nash and his wife Alicia, and directed by Marymount parent, Ron Howard.*

Members of the Marymount Singers at the annual Christmas Fair

Members of the Class of 2002 with Beth Nielsen Werwaiss '61, 75th Anniversary Chair,
enjoying birthday cake following the closing liturgy of the 75th anniversary

Commencement 2001. On Tuesday, June 12, at the Church of St. Ignatius Loyola, the 39 members of the Class of 2001
became the seventy-third class to graduate from Marymount School. On the evening before graduation,
a Baccalaureate Mass and Reception honoring each senior has become a tradition.

Reflections from the Closing Liturgy of the 75th Anniversary Year

". . . 2001 was an important year for Marymount, and we will remember it as the year of the 75th Anniversary and the red, white and blue balloons that filled Fifth Avenue. However, 2001 will also be remembered as the year our world changed. But somehow, in the midst of sheer calamity and fear for the future, we upheld our spirit that did become a light that shined in the darkness. This amazing spirit remained present from September 11th to the Rockaway tragedy to turkey baskets to the toy drive to today, as we gather together to celebrate. As we close the 75th year and bridge our way into the 76th, we carry with us our school's history, Mother Butler's vision, and the spirit that is instilled within each and every one of us. God has provided us with numerous blessings throughout our past, which has given us hope for the future. Marymount's 76th year marks the opening of 2 East 82nd Street, and, together, the four buildings will continue to educate and produce independent young women who can challenge a world that is always changing, the type of women we are on our way to becoming. And though we can't physically stay here forever, spiritually we remain a part of the community called Marymount, a place like no other."

PRIANY HADIATMODJO '02

Sr. Kathleen Fagan (left), and Mary Ellen Gozdecki, headmistress of the Marymount School in Los Angeles (far right), with Upper School students in front of a banner created by Marymount L.A. students. The banner includes messages of support and was part of a care package that was sent to the Marymount School community in response to the events of September 11, 2001.

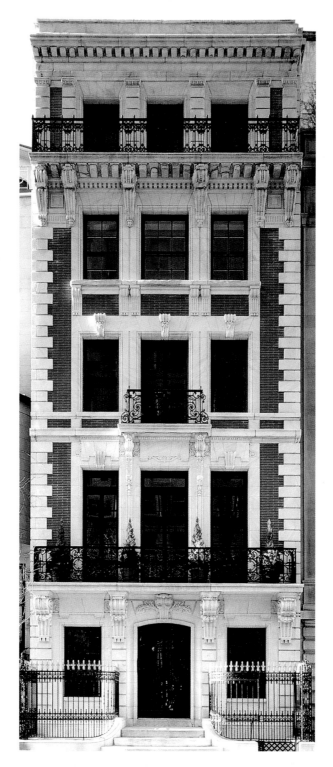

Marymount Middle School, 2 East 82nd Street

B Y THE late 1990s, Marymount was already planning its move into the twenty-first century and the celebration of its 75th anniversary in 2001.

These milestones came at a time when there was renewed recognition of the importance of single-sex education, especially for preadolescent and adolescent girls. Much recent research documents ways in which females are overlooked in the coed environment. The National Coalition of Girls' Schools, of which Marymount is a member reports that in a 1999 survey of more than 4000 alumnae from girls' schools, an overwhelming majority felt their schools provided superior academic education, instilled self-confidence, and gave them an advantage in choosing a college and taking on leadership roles.

For Marymount, the value of such education is neither a new discovery nor a new commitment. In 1926, when Mother Butler founded Marymount, the total acceptance of women as engineers, physicians, architects, and senators was remote. Mother Butler's mission of providing a challenging, high-quality education for young women and girls was ahead of its time, and for 75 years, the excellence of a Marymount education has shaped the lives of generations of women. Marymount graduates have indeed distinguished themselves as leaders in education, law, the arts, business, government, medicine, and community affairs. Today, when women are still underrepresented in science, math, and technology, Marymount has made an enormous investment in providing the highest quality facilities and instruction in these areas, while continuing to offer the finest education in the arts and humanities.

Key elements of this education include a personal approach grounded in the understanding that each student has her own unique style of learning, and a Catholic heritage that informs the moral and spiritual

Chapter Eleven: THE FUTURE

development of students. Young women graduate from Marymount with the intellectual discipline, cultural sensitivity, global perspective and ethical values to succeed as leaders and problem solvers of the twenty-first century. As Erin McDermott, the Valedictorian of the Class of 2001, stated: "We are . . . strong, independent, sophisticated, and inspired young women who will dare to risk, challenge and truly shape the world."

In the spring of 1997, with these strengths as a foundation, the Board of Trustees established a Strategic Planning Committee and retained an experienced consultant on independent school planning. In January 1998, the trustees and representatives of the school's major constituencies participated in a three-day planning session to evaluate the school's programs and facilities and to create a plan for the future. A task force studied the question of enrollment and recommended that while individual class size remain small, overall enrollment be increased to 500 students across all grade levels in order to provide for an expanded curriculum. Marymount's Strategic Plan, approved by the Board in 1998, outlined goals, rationale, and strategies for implementation in the areas of educational program, student population, staff, parents and alumnae, governance, communications, plant, finance and development. The Strategic Plan states: "Recognizing the challenges and possibilities that the twenty-first century will present, Marymount School will continue to educate girls through a rigorous academic program designed to encourage critical and creative thinking and to promote independent inquiry. The School, through a college-preparatory curriculum, will maintain a balanced program that fosters the spiritual, intellectual, aesthetic and physical development of our students and places a strong emphasis on moral and social responsibility. Marymount will continue to offer each girl opportunities for leadership and collaboration, preparing her for an active role in a changing world."

In addition to its own Strategic Plan, Marymount School of New York has collaborated with other Marymount Schools in the United States and Europe to ensure that the school's RSHM heritage will continue to inform its future, even if, at some point, there are no RSHM on the staff. In March 1999, Sister Kathleen Fagan, Headmistress; Dr. Jane Haher-Izquierdo, President of the Board of Trustees; Pat Barter, Associate Headmistress; and Concepcion Alvar, Director of Admissions, met in Béziers, France with representatives of other Marymount Schools to immerse themselves in the history, charism and spirituality of the original founders of the Religious of the Sacred Heart of Mary. A set of Goals and Criteria has been established for the network of Marymount Schools, to ensure that the founding mission of the RSHM will continue in the future. Various members of Marymount's faculty have attended meetings held in London, England, and Nice, France. Still other faculty members have visited Béziers and met with faculty from other Marymount Schools. Ideally, every faculty member will eventually have the opportunity for a "Béziers experience." Meanwhile, at each of the network schools, implementation teams have been active in assessing the ways in which the school fulfills the network's goals, which are to foster a personal relationship with God, to create unity through diversity, to instill a life-long love of learning, to encourage and affirm personal growth, to awaken a consciousness of social justice, and to fulfill the RSHM mission "that all may have life." Marymount's Board of Trustees, administrators, and faculty have enthusiastically embraced this opportunity and responsibility to carry on the RSHM legacy.

As the new millennium approached, the Board of Trustees also began an active search for a new school facility, and in August 1999, the school announced the purchase of a *beaux arts* building at 2 East 82nd Street to serve as the future home of the Middle School. Marymount's renovation of the building will leave intact many of its special architectural features and, at the same time, provide additional space in both school locations for library, music, science, art, drama, computer, and dining facilities. The proximity of the new site to the present school will ensure continued interaction and a sense of community. At the same time, the unique needs of the young adolescent will be more effectively addressed when the Middle School has its own building.

With the Strategic Plan in place and the acquisition of the new building assured, the Board of Trustees launched The Campaign For Marymount. Its three main goals are to create a Middle School at the new building, 2 East 82nd Street, to redesign the Fifth Avenue buildings to optimize the use of classrooms, homerooms and labs that will become available when the Middle School relocates, and to increase endowment for faculty compensation, financial aid opportunities, technology support, and the maintenance of the beautiful buildings.

As Marymount closes its 75th anniversary year and embarks on its newest projects, the school reaffirms its commitment to the vision of Mother Butler; to educate girls and young women in a challenging, supportive, and structured learning environment. As Christiane Gannon of the Class of 2001 affirmed in her reflections at the 75th Anniversary Mass of Thanksgiving, "The kind of 'total growth' that Mother Butler envisioned happens only in . . . a place where you can live, laugh, learn and love, where you can make mistakes and be forgiven, where you may build a foundation for your dreams, and where no dream is ever labeled impossible. Over the past seventy-five years, Marymount has given her students remarkable gifts . . . empowering knowledge, the

courage to live a full life in our changing world [and] the strength of voice needed to make a difference in that world."

As the traffic on Fifth Avenue stopped and balloons soared into the air and the anniversary flag was raised for Founder's Day 2001, Marymount School celebrated seventy-five extraordinary years. From its founding in the Roaring Twenties, through the Depression and war years of the 1930s and 1940s, the changing times of the 1960s and 1970s, the expansion of the 1980s and 1990s, into its bright future in the new millennium, Marymount has remained faithful to its mission as an outstanding independent Catholic day school dedicated to academic excellence and religious values.

"In 1926 our Founders recognized the importance of educating young women; today our mission remains constant. I firmly believe that we engage and empower our students with knowledge, critical thinking and social conscience, and they thereby develop their unique strengths and a deep sense of who they are before God. They will lead our global community."

Kathleen Fagan, RSHM '59
Headmistress

A Tribute to Faculty and Staff

WHEN THE Strategic Planning Committee met in 1998 and charted the future of the school, there was unanimous recognition that central to an outstanding school is a dedicated and professional staff. A priority of the Strategic Plan that evolved from the Committee's work was that the school continue to attract, recruit and retain the most highly qualified teaching and administrative staff. And so it has always been at Marymount School.

When the school opened in 1926 there was a staff of six RSHM and at least two lay teachers. Until the 1960s, teaching and administrative faculty were nearly all members of the religious order with only a few lay teachers, often teaching physical education, foreign language or an occasional "special" program. Male faculty were not found in numbers at the school until recent years.

Marymount has been blessed with extraordinary faculty and staff. Through the years they have shared their intelligence, talents, energies, and spirit with Marymount students. The myriad of activities remembered in this book reflect their work—the planning, implementing and seeking the "teachable moment" in every student project, every academic or sports competition, every production, every sacrament, every celebration throughout the seventy-five years of Marymount's history. From planning the details of taking a nursery class to see the Christmas tree at The Metropolitan Museum of Art to ordering the red roses for the graduates to carry at commencement, there are thousands of moments every year when faculty and staff are the willing hands and loving minds that provide the best possible learning experience for Marymount students.

We cannot list them all but have been reminded by alumnae, in the course of preparation for this book, of many wonderful teachers and staff through the years who have made such a difference in students' lives. We remember the many extra hours before, during and after school when teachers willingly gave of their time. We remember the many faculty and administrators who have served as greeters in the morning, giving students the first smile of many that they receive each day. We remember the early teachers of technology who first had to teach themselves about the new computer phenomena and then guide students and faculty through the technology "revolution." We remember hundreds of sports competitions that Marymount students have participated in and the hours and hours of preparation and organization that faculty and coaches have given to maximize student opportunities. We remember the academic competitions our students have participated in—the hours of coaching for Model United Nations, Mock Trial, Shakespeare performance events, and many, many others for which teachers have given personal time to make student participation possible. We remember the countless everyday celebrations for which the RSHM Sisters, in years gone by, and lay staff, in recent times, have provided refreshments for students, parents, alumnae and administrators; the custodians who have done the room setups for the dozens of events that occur in Marymount School in any week and the staff who have helped to maintain the beauty and cleanliness of the Marymount environment. We remember the yearbooks and student newspapers through the years produced with faculty guidance; the school trips, the exchange programs and the retreats planned with careful faculty and administrative attention. The Halloween haunted houses, the skits and the famous "Twelve Days of Christmas"(just before students leave for Christmas holidays) are some fun events, among many, conceived by administrators, faculty and staff to enrich the Marymount experience for all.

Throughout its history faculty and staff have been a vital thread in the tapestry that is Marymount School. It is to them that this book is dedicated.

Longtime staff members Dorothy Surella, who came to the school in 1968 and Susana Acosta, who joined the staff in 1962

Current Faculty and Staff Who Have Served at Marymount School for Ten or More Years:

Susana Acosta	Kathleen Fagan, RSHM	Pam Masturzo
Concepcion Alvar	Johanna Fleming	Maggie Devany McKee
Monika Anderson	Annette Hayde	Luiz Montanez
Itir Arkan	Susan Johnson	Venetia Oliver
Pat Barter	Virginia Kenney	Armando Perez
Anne Considine, RSHM	Catherine Koller	Dorothy Surella
Donna Corvi	Ann Lanza	George Ulloa
Linda Dindorf	Barbara Ledig-Sheehan	Clevie Youngblood, RSHM

RSHM who currently serve with
Sister Kathleen Fagan at Marymount School

Sister Anne Considine (left), and Sister Clevie Youngblood, Commencement, 2000

Sister Anne Considine, RSHM

Born in County Clare, Ireland, Sister Anne's early education was at the Cree National School and the Convent of Mercy in Kilrush, County Clare. She entered the RSHM community in 1953 at Tarrytown, New York. Sister Anne received a Bachelor of Arts degree from Marymount College in Tarrytown in 1960 and a Master's Degree in Mathematical Scholarship from New York University in 1970. From the mid-fifties until the 1980s, Sr. Anne taught at schools including St. Thomas Aquinas School, Mother Butler Memorial High School and Sacred Heart of Mary School–all in the Bronx, New York and at Saint Gregory's in Manhattan. She taught mathematics at the College of New Resources Division of New Rochelle College in the South Bronx and at Marymount Manhattan College. She has been on the Mathematics faculty at Marymount School since 1982.

Sister Clevie Youngblood, RSHM

Though born in New York City, Sr. Clevie's early education took place at Saint Rita's School and Marymount School in Arlington after her family moved to Virginia. Sister Clevie received her Bachelor of Arts Degree in History from The College of William and Mary and entered the Religious of the Sacred Heart of Mary in 1967 in Arlington. She received a Master's Degree in Social Studies and Education from City College of New York in 1978, a Graduate Certificate in Biblical Spirituality from the Chicago Theological Union in 1989 and a Master's Degree in Religious Education from Fordham University in 1990. She has taught at Saint John's Elementary School in McLean, Virginia, at the two RSHM schools in the Bronx, Mother Butler Memorial High School and Sacred Heart of Mary High School. Sr. Clevie has also served as Assistant Director for Advisement at Marymount Manhattan College. In 1979, she came to Marymount School and served as head of Upper School. In 1985, she was transferred to the Marymount International School, Rome, serving as Academic Dean for three years. From 1990 to the present, Sr. Clevie has served as Chair of the Religious Studies Department at Marymount School.

Members of the RSHM who have served at Marymount School

Presently Serving
Sr. Anne Considine
Sr. Kathleen Fagan
Sr. Clevie Youngblood

Served in the Past
Sr. Catherine (des Anges) Bennett
Sr. Majella Berg
Sr. Alice Melchior Biegen
Sr. Consilia Boran
Sr. Veronica Brand
Sr. Madeleine Cain
Sr. Barbara Carvalho
Sr. Joan Regis Catherwood
Sr. Irene Cody
Sr. William Daly
Sr. Catherine Deubel
Sr. Virginia Dorgan
Sr. Patricia (Timothy) Fahey
Sr. Theresa Fahey
Sr. Teresita Fay
Sr. Paulina Ferrao
Sr. Agnes Fleming
Sr. Martin Fleming
Sr. Elizabeth Gallagher
Sr. Scholastica Gonzalez
Sr. Albert Higgins
Sr. Gertrude Higgins
Sr. Anne Marie (des Victoires) Hill
Sr. Mary Lang
Sr. Georgette Lawton
Sr. Edna (Henri) Lutton
Sr. Christine Marion
Sr. Teresa Martin
Sr. Raymunde McKay
Sr. Raphael McKenny
Sr. Marguerite McLoughlin
Sr. Colette McManus
Sr. Lucille Melo
Sr. des Victoires Moran
Sr. Genevieve Murphy
Sr. Rosaleen O'Halloran
Sr. Marie (St. Clement) O'Malley
Sr. Catherine Mary Patten
Sr. Filomena Peixioto
Sr. Jacquelyn Porter
Sr. Josephine (Alphonsus) Rooney
Sr. Breda Shelly

Sr. Rosaleen (Kostka) Sheridan
Sr. Alphonsine Tyrrell
Sr. Maureen Vellon
Sr. Inez Vieira
Sr. Assunta Villamil
Sr. Mary Catherine (Berchmans) Walsh
Sr. Margaret (Ferdinand) Wiener
Sr. Mary Alice Young

Deceased
Sr. Antoine Campbell
Sr. Mary Therese Coleman
Sr. Marie du Carmel Connolly
Sr. Therese Dalton
Sr. de Lourdes Dillan
Sr. Aiden Doran
Sr. Cecelia Duffy
Sr. Agnes de Jesus Elliot
Sr. Edmund Harvey
Sr. Louise Hogan
Sr. Antoinette Joyce
Sr. Fidelma Keaney
Sr. Ignatius Kearney
Sr. Patricia Lacey
Sr. Anthony Lynch
Sr. Angela Martin
Sr. Winifred McConville
Sr. Evangelist McGucken
Sr. Mary McHugh
Sr. Christopher McInerney
Sr. Leo McKallagat
Sr. Immaculee McMullen
Sr. Dolorita Mooney
Sr. Presentation Murphy
Sr. Clementine Murray
Sr. Martha Mythen
Sr. Barbara O'Connor
Sr. Josephine O'Hara
Sr. Aiden O'Sullivan
Sr. Bernard Quinn
Sr. Cecilia Rafter
Sr. San Juan Romero
Sr. Rita Rowley
Sr. Brigid Rowsome
Sr. St. James Ruddy
Sr. Patricia Sauer
Sr. Catherine Staudermann
Sr. Jean Baptiste Steinbugler
Sr. Genevieve Toner
Sr. Adrian Walsh

Some Historical Highlights: A Marymount Timeline

1849 The Religious of the Sacred Heart of Mary (RSHM) is founded by Père Jean Antoine Gailhac and Mère St. Jean Pelissier-Cure.

1860 Johanna Butler is born in Kilkenny, Ireland. She enters the novitiate of the RSHM in Béziers, France, at the age of sixteen and takes the name Marie Joseph.

1877 The first group of RSHM comes to the United States. Their first ministry is at Sag Harbor, New York.

1903 Mother Butler is assigned to the United States and embarks on her life's work as a leader in American education.

1906 Mother Butler's cousin James supports her dream of establishing a school to educate young women and girls. He purchases the Reynard estate in Tarrytown and deeds it to the RSHM.

1907 Mother Butler and the RSHM sisters convert the mansion, situated high on a hill overlooking the Hudson River, into a school, and call the new school Marymount.

1923 Mother Butler opens schools in Paris and Los Angeles.

1925 In response to the need expressed by the Tarrytown alumnae for a school for their children in New York City, Mother Butler purchases 1028 Fifth Avenue from Florence Vanderbilt-Burden on December 31, 1925.

1926 RSHM sisters arrive after New Year's Day to begin converting the 1028 mansion into a school. On February 2, the school is dedicated. Mother Ignatius Kearney is placed in charge of the school. Mother Butler is elected General Superior of the International Congregation of the Religious of the Sacred Heart of Mary.

1928 The first yearbook, the *Marifia,* is published. The name is a contraction of Marymount Fifth Avenue.

1930 Istituto Marymount Rome is founded.

1935 The Alumnae Association is established.

1936 At the height of the Great Depression, Marymount School celebrates its tenth anniversary and purchases the Herbert Pratt mansion at 1027 Fifth Avenue. The Mothers' Auxiliary is formed.

1940 Mother Butler dies on April 23. Her body is interred in the crypt beneath the Butler Memorial Chapel, Marymount Convent, Tarrytown.

1946 Marymount is accredited by the University of the State of New York. The first issue of the *Joritan*, the student newspaper, is published. The name is a contraction of the names Joseph and Rita, honoring

Mother Joseph Butler and Mother Rita Rowley. Marymount International School is founded in Rome.

1950 The Dunlevy Milbank mansion at 1026 Fifth Avenue is acquired, providing the necessary space for a full academic program from pre-kindergarten through Class XII.

1956 Marymount in Umtali, Rhodesia (now Zimbabwe) opens.

1966 The *Marifia* Chapter of the National Honor Society is formed.

1969 Marymount is independently incorporated and governed by a Board of Trustees.

1976 Marymount celebrates its 50th Anniversary.

1977 The Metropolitan Museum Historic District is designated by the Landmarks Preservation Commission, protecting Marymount as part of a landmarked district.

1978 The first computers for student use are installed at Marymount.

1984 A gymnasium on top of the three Fifth Avenue buildings is completed, allowing Marymount to expand its athletic offerings and interscholastic teams.

1986 Marymount celebrates its 60th Anniversary.

1989 A Middle School division is created.

1994 A new science center opens.

1996 The Marymount Web site is created and becomes a portal for student learning on the Internet.

1997 The Board of Trustees establishes a Strategic Planning Committee to plan for the future of Marymount School.

1998 Fifty-three members of the Marymount community, including parents, faculty, alumnae, administrators and trustees, meet in January at a three-day conference to design a Strategic Plan for the school. In June, the goals of the Plan are approved by the Board of Trustees.

1999 Marymount purchases a building at 2 East 82nd Street to serve as the future home of the Middle School.

2000 The Landmarks Preservation Commission approves the plan for the new Middle School.

2001 Marymount celebrates its 75th Anniversary.

APPENDICES

STATEMENT OF MISSION

Marymount School of New York is an independent, Catholic, day school founded to educate girls in a tradition of academic excellence and moral values. The school promotes in each student a respect for her own unique abilities and a commitment to responsible living in a changing world. Marymount welcomes diversity and draws upon it to foster cultural sensitivity, religious understanding and a global perspective. Embracing the full spectrum of development from Nursery to Class XII, the school affirms the value of educating the whole child in a challenging, supportive and structured learning environment.

Central to the mission of the school is the academic enterprise - the acquisition of knowledge and the development of life-long skills of critical thinking and clear expression. Emphasizing classic disciplines and scientific inquiry, the college preparatory curriculum also includes a varied program of athletics as well as the aesthetic and performing arts. Each student is encouraged to approach learning as a continuing, dynamic and rewarding adventure.

A wide range of activities complements the academic program and increases opportunities for creativity, self-expression, competition and collaboration. These experiences foster social skills, sportsmanship, a sense of responsibility, independence and self-confidence.

The religious traditions of the school provide a foundation for articulating and exploring questions of personal integrity, ethical decision-making and social justice. Committed to its Catholic heritage, Marymount values the religious diversity of its community and seeks to give students of every faith a deeper understanding of the role of the spiritual in life and an appreciation of individual religious traditions.

We appreciate the separate yet interlocking roles of parents, students and staff in building the community. Parents are recognized and respected as the primary educators of their child. Teachers strive to know each of their students well, to respond to individual needs and to encourage initiative and accomplishment. Students are urged to become active community participants responsive to others within and beyond Marymount.

In sum, Marymount seeks to educate young women who continue to question, risk and grow—young women who care, serve and lead—young women prepared to challenge, shape and change the world.

RSHM Mission Statement

"That All May Have Life"

We, the Religious of the Sacred Heart of Mary, an international apostolic institute of women religious, are called to share in the life-giving mission of Jesus Christ.

The challenge of the gospel and the spirit of faith and zeal which marked our founders, Jean Gailhac and Mere St. Jean, and our founding sisters, urge us to respond to the needs of our time and to work with others in action for evangelical justice. Sent to promote the life and dignity of all our sisters and brothers, at this time we place ourselves and our resources at the service of those who are most in need of justice, enabling the powerless, the deprived, the marginalized, the voiceless to work effectively for their own development and liberation.

We are called to be community, to know and celebrate God's love for us and to make that love known to others. As we become more deeply inserted in the realities of the Church and the world, we use our individual and corporate talents to work creatively in diverse ministries for the promotion of justice.

Mary is our model as we seek to be open to the Spirit, to center our lives in Jesus Christ, to be women of prayer and compassion, and to give authentic and joyful witness to the values of the gospel wherever we are.

(Ratified by the General Chapter, Rome, 1990)

Goals

A Marymount School is a community that commits itself:

1. To foster a personal relationship with God.
2. To create unity through diversity.
3. To instill a life-long love of learning.
4. To encourage and affirm personal growth.
5. To awaken a consciousness of social justice.
6. To fulfill the RSHM mission–"That all may have life."

Marymount Network of Schools

Universities and Colleges

Loyola Marymount University, Los Angeles, California
Marymount College, Palos Verdes, California
Marymount College, Tarrytown, New York
Marymount Manhattan College, New York, New York
Marymount University, Arlington, Virginia

Elementary and Middle Schools

Marymount School, New York, New York
Marymount School, Neuilly, Paris, France
Marymount International School, Rome, Italy
Istituto Marymount, Rome, Italy

Secondary Schools

Marymount High School, Los Angeles, California
Marymount School, New York, New York
Marymount International School, Kingston-on-Thames, Surrey, England
Marymount International School, Rome, Italy

Board of Trustees May, 2001

Alumnae and Parent Associations Leadership

When the school governance was transferred to a Board of Trustees in 1969, the organization of Alumnae and Parents' Associations was discussed. In 1975, the presidents of both groups became "ex officio" members of the Board of Trustees for the length of their terms. The following have served in the years since incorporation.

Presidents of the Alumnae Association

1969	Cornelia Ladas Bauer Iredell '55
1971	Maryellen McGoldrick Schwarz '56
1975	Mary Jane McCabe Belt '58
1978	Marta Montanez Casals Istomin '54
1980	Jane Haher-Izquierdo, MD '58
1987	Cathy Sattenstein Callender '60
1997	Beth Nielsen Werwaiss '61

Presidents of the Parents' Association

1970-72	C. Stephen Connolly, MD
1972-74	James T. DeLuca, MD
1974-76	Terry Vickers
1976-77	Tennant Glenn-Davitian
1977-78	Carol Simpson
1978-79	Pat Barter
1979-81	Kathleen Harshberger
1981-83	Annette Hayde
1983-85	Diane Held Segalas
1985-87	Nancy Cuttita
1987-88	Irene Flowers
1988-90	Kathy Borkowski
1990-92	Francine Jacques
1992-94	Carol Ryan
1994-96	Lynn Harvey
1996-98	Mary Lollis
1998-00	Patti Simone
2000-02	Christine Danielewski

Capital Campaign Leadership

The Campaign for the Gymnasium

Campaign Chair
John Pero

Special Gifts Committee Chair
Robert L. Henkle

Alumnae Chair
Ann C. Scavullo '63

Director of Capital Campaign
Pat Barter

The Campaign for Science

Honorary Chairs
Sister Antoine Campbell, RSHM
Sister Elizabeth Gallagher, RSHM
Charles Grace
A. Robert Towbin
Hugo Gelardin

Campaign Co-Chairs
Erika K. and Peter Aron
Diane and Spiros Segalas

Trustee Chair
Robert L. Henkle

Alumnae Chair
Catherine Callender '60

Past Parent Chair
Luba Corso

Parent Co-Chairs
Diane and Frank Kaufman

Director of Campaign for Science
Pat Barter

The Campaign For Marymount

Honorary Chairs:
Erika K. and Peter Aron
Margaret and Charles M. Grace
Noriko and Susumu Maeda
Diane and Spiros Segalas
Jacqueline and A. Robert Towbin

Campaign Co-Chairs
Cynthia and Dennis A. Suskind
Alison and Boniface Zaino

Steering Committee:
Erika K. Aron
Barbara Bricker '54
Francis Dunleavy
Kathleen Fagan, RSHM '59
Patricia Moore Fisher '60
Kathleen Harshberger
Catherine Hohenlohe Jacobus '60
Mary Lisanti '74
John W. Lombardo, MD
Prema Mathai-Davis, PhD
Edward McLaughlin
Robert Reuben
Barbara Weisz
Beth Nielsen Werwaiss '61
Deborah Wiley

Director of Development
Cathy Callender '60

Pat Barter

*Dennis Suskind and Alison Zaino,
Campaign For Marymount Co-Chairs*

Erika Talbot Award

Erika Talbot was born on September 3, 1961. She entered Marymount kindergarten on September 21, 1966. At the time she was suffering from cerebral palsy. Erika died in 1971 at the age of nine. In 1972 Marymount instituted an award in her memory. The award was given to students in the following classes who demonstrated outstanding cooperation with teachers and classmates.

The recipients of this award have been:

1972
Class VII	Valerie Stern
Class VI	Margaret Mary Edsall
Class V	Carmina del Rosario
Class IV	Maria Sozzani
Class III	Jill Rukeyser
Class II	Margaret Putman
Class I	Casey Napoli

1973
Class VIII	Peggy Pogue
Class VII	Katherine Mitchell
Class VI	Nicolette Abysalh
Class V	Elizabeth Seidman
Class IV	Toni Kotite
Class III	Elizabeth Latchford
Class II	Muriel Bell
Class I	Gabrielle Marroig-Tagle

1974
Class VII	Aurea George
Class VI	Alice Tepper
Class V	Elizabeth Moritz
Class IV	April Castle
Class III	Paula Maria Pacheco
Class II	Kristina Curtis
Class I	Eva Cugini

1975
Class VI	Dorian Deglin
Class V	Jennifer Howland
Class IV	Laura Moritz
Class III	Jenny Federman
Class II	Christine Thelmo
Class I	Jocelyn Santos

1976
Class VIII	Alexandra Chipurnoi
Class VII	Toni Kotite
Class VI	April Castle
Class V	Jeanmarie Ermelino
Class IV	Elizabeth Howland
Sr. Genevieve's Class	Yana Nezhdanov
Mrs. Whalley's Class	Tara Gardner

1977
Class VI	Mary Jane MacGuire
Class V	Mary Dorrian
Class IV	Anya MacMahon
Ms. Battaglia's Class	Karin Marie Fittante
Mrs. Ramsey's Class	Veronica Carrillo

1978
Class VI	Stefania Viola
Class V	Daniele Napoli
Class IV	Jocelyn Santos
Class III	Veronica Carrillo
Class II	Katina Pearl
Class I	Philona Rowell

1979
Class VI	Shelley Carter
Class V	Stacey Rynn
Class IV	Jennifer Rockford
Class III	Jennifer Katz
Class II	Miranda Hambro
Class I	Deirdre Gugelot

1980
Class VI	Elizabeth Millstein
Class V	Erin Harshberger
Class IV	Alexandra Franco
Class III	Christina Errazuriz
Class II	Angela Pulecio
Class I	Deirdre Dugan

1981
Class VI	Alexandra Pero
Class V	Paula Baraona
Class IV	Philana Rowell
Class III	Samantha Salcedo
Class II	Siobain Fisher
Class I	Alessandra Herbosch

1982
Class VI	Michelle Joseph
Class V	Elizabeth Harris
Class IV	Filipa Tierno
Class III	Emilie Schreiner
Class II	Manola Moretti
Class I	Claire Mathis

1983
Class VI	Philana Rowell
Class V	Giulia Caltagirone
Class IV	Siobain Fisher
Class III	Melody Brynner
Class II	Jamie McLoughlin
Class I	Christina Zaloum

1984

Class VI	Filipa Tierno
Class V	Soon-Ye Farrow-Previn
Class IV	Manola Moretti
Class III	Meredith Spungin
Class II	Mari-Claudia Jimenez
Class I	Andrea Zaloum

1985

Class VI	Monica Corso
Class V	Sheila Suzara
Class IV	Jamie McLoughlin
Class III	Angel Neelankavil
Class II	Abigail Feerick
Class I	Elizabeth Ryan

1986

Class VI	Gillian Peterson
Class V	Michelle Johns
Class IV	Jennifer Suzara
Class III	Cara Grabowski

1987

Class VI	Meredith Spungin
Class V	Angel Neelankavil
Class IV	Maria Papadopoulos
Class III	Reshma Vaswani

1988

Class VI	Angel Neelankavil
Class V	Vanessa Meola
Class IV	Laura Pietropinto
Class III	Nora Czuchlewski

1989

Class VI	Brigida San Martin
Class V	Reshma Vaswani
Class IV	Monica San Martin
Class III	Jennifer Clark

1990

Class VII	Leslie Koo
Class VI	Victoria Tudella
Class V	Echo Aoki
Class IV	Aarti Vaswani

1991

Class VII	Misha Wright
Class VI	Canem Arkan
Class V	Laura DiLauro
Class IV	Holly Aron

1992

Class VII	Madzia Bartkowiak
Class VI	Christina Bianco
Class V	Helena Marrin

1993

Class VII	Kristin Lollis
Class VI	Katrina Coddington
Class V	Begona Sebastian
Class IV	Alexandra Reboul

1994

Class VII	Dana Iannuzzi
Class VI	Kristin Klein
Class V	Julia Bianco
Class IV	Priany Hadiatmodjo

1995

Class VII	Eve Gibson
Class VI	Kelly Murray
Class V	Alexis Markel
Class IV	Heather Wild

1996

Class VII	Annie Yoon
Class VI	Margie Gorman
Class V	Megan Erpf
Class IV	Emi Bratt

1997

Class VII	Sarah Jordan
Class VI	Ashley Fairey
Class V	Kristin Hoeberlein
Class IV	Irina Navasardian

1998

Class VII	Shanee Brown
Class VI	Katherine Duncan
Class V	Maria Giovanna Guinchard
Class IV	Chiara Ravalli

1999

Class VII	Olivia Whelan
Class VI	Kiera O'Shea
Class V	Darley Maw
Class IV	Anna Sherman

2000

Class VII	Chelsea Hess
Class VI	Leslie Lim
Class V	Ashley Cox
Class IV	Silvia Callegari

2001

Class VII	Jacqueline Bessey
Class VI	Melody Nath
Class V	Claude Adjile
Class IV	Charlotte Hauser

Sister Antoine Campbell Award

The Marymount School Alumnae Association in 1978, established an award to honor Sister Antoine Campbell, to commemorate her fifty years of service as a Religious of the Sacred Heart of Mary. Sister Antoine, who died in 1998, first came to Marymount in 1929, just three years after the school was founded, and she spent more than thirty years in a variety of positions at the School—as a teacher of Latin and speech, headmistress and director of alumnae relations. Each year, the senior class and the faculty vote for the student who exemplifies the qualities which Sister Antoine brought to Marymount. The award is given to the graduate who, through her generosity, kindness and openness to others has fostered a sense of spirit in her class and in her School, and demonstrated a concern for the entire human family.

The recipients of this award have been:

1978	Lauren-Glenn Davitian	1990	Sandra Carreon
	Amanda Neal	1991	Monica Corso
1979	Jean Bambury	1992	Jeanette Enriquez
1980	Maureen Carmody	1993	Monica Baisley
1981	Ellen Dunn	1994	Kelly Mahoney
1982	Jacqueline Galatola		Dennise Mulvihill
	Sarah Grossi	1995	Jennifer Dwyer
1983	Margaret Farrell	1996	Ann Marie Benitez
1984	Christine Murphy		Laura Pietropinto
1985	Christine Toner	1997	Jennifer Heger
1986	Adrienne Giacinto		Jade Williams
	Jocelyn Santos	1998	Stephanie Brosnahan
1987	Maria Corey		Alicia Stoller
	Nancy Cuttita	1999	Katherine Rosenblatt
1988	Katina Pearl	2000	Alessandra Assante
1989	Elizabeth Crotty	2001	Julia Bianco
	Rita Pietropinto		

Heather Hertzan Award

The Parents' Association sponsors the Heather Hertzan Award to honor the memory of Heather who died in September 1994. The award, open to all Lower, Middle and Upper School students is given out at the closing ceremonies of the school year. The award is given to a student who exemplifies Heather's qualities of enthusiastic participation in school life; who through her active involvement in learning activities and extracurricular activities contributes to the spirit of community at Marymount.

The recipients of this award have been:

1995	Julia Bianco
1996	Misha Wright
1997	Antonia Abram
1998	Dana Iannuzzi
1999	Miriam Ritchie
2000	Yi Zheng
2001	Audrey Suskind

Heather Hertzan

TRAILBLAZER AWARD

As part of the 75th Anniversary Year, Marymount held its first Homecoming in January 2001, established the Trailblazer Award and inducted student athletes onto the newly created Wall of Fame. In 2001, athletes from 1980-1994 were recognized and in 2002, those from 1995 and 1996.

...until 1995

This award honors alumnae from the Class of 1980 through the Class of 1994 who distinguished themselves on Marymount's athletic teams and in doing so "have been among the athletes who have changed the way the world views women's sports."

1995 and later...

Marymount recognizes and honors its recent athletes who have distinguished themselves within the Athletic Association of Independent Schools. These athletes have succeeded in competition at a very high level and have set themselves apart not only within Marymount but in the entire league as well.

The recipients of this award have been:

Lissa Degnan '80
Alina Herrera '81
Pamela Kenny '82
Christine Murphy '84
Anya MacMahon '85
Melissa Phelan '85
Kendra Freehill '86
Jennifer Katz '88
Elisabeth Harvey Bull '89
Chiara Hausmann '89
Deborah Misir '89
Mary Beth Williams '89
Nicole Benjamin '90
Sandra Carreon '90
Alicia Guevara '90
Mary Ellen Lennon '90
Jeanette Enriquez '92
Jocelyn Cortez '93

Kerry Ann DaCosta '93
Tania Mariani '93
Ana Maria Perkovic '93
Daphne Segalas '93
Jennia White '93
Katherine Nastro '94
Natasha Archer '95
Ingrid Cubillos '95
Kathy Cosgrove '95
Teresa McNamara '95
Maria Papadopoulos '95
Jean Quinn '95
Bababunmi Adelana '96
Mia Alvar '96
Izabela Grocholski '96
Deborah Harvey '96
Brooke McLean '96
Tara Shanahan '96

Trailblazers, 2001

Trailblazers, 2002

ATHLETIC DIRECTOR'S AWARD
(Established in 2002)

This award is given at Homecoming to a first-year college student who was of particular assistance to the Athletic Department while at Marymount.

First Recipient

Kaylan Scagliola '01

Susana Acosta
Jane Amorosi '61
Maureen Armstrong Allegaert '50
Kathleen Birkey
Barbara Bricker '54
Veronique Firkusny Callegari '84
Patsy Cooper and Warren Frisina
Debra Corcoran
Michelle Cox '89
Kathy and John Crosson
Kelly DeMarco
Kathleen O'Shea Donohue '63
Dr. Jeanne Baker Driscoll
Margaret Dunleavy
Maureen Flynn '64
Shauna and John Gallagher
Genevieve Gleason
Mary-Ann Lynch Goldstein '58
June Gumbel
Vicki Guranowski Har-Even '67
Kathleen Harshberger
Ann Harrison

Lynn Harvey
Tamara Hallisey Hatfield '76
Rosemary Heath '70
Patricia Hehman '79
Justine Hopper '79
Marjorie Ihrig '53
Jayne and Titus Kana
Anne Marie Keyes '56
Christina Krupka '64
Alix and John Lombardo
Melissa Loughlin
Lydia Mannara '70
Belinda Markel
Adrian Martin-Wat '75
Alana McGrattan '62
Nordal McWethy
Marion Monachelli
Valery Shields Moore '59
Caroline Nastro '88
Marilyn E. Noz '57
Mary Papadopoulos
Linda and Joseph Perrotta

Rita Pietropinto-Kitt '89
Ann Dillon Priolo '60
Dr. Elena Quevedo-Chigas
Flaminia Ravalli
Joanne Safian, RSHM '64
Carmen San Miguel
Carmencita San Miguel '91
Vera Scanlon '86
Maryellen McGoldrick Schwarz '56
Mary Selover
Mary Hartel Semack '84
Constance Dunkin Smith '77
Dorothy Surella
Cynthia Suskind
Mary A. Taylor
Karen Tompkins
Kathryn Toohig '64
Joanne Czechlewski Wallace '63 and
William Wallace
Beth Nielsen Werwaiss '61
Ralph Yznaga

*Some members of the 75th Anniversary
Archives Committee at work*

INDEX

Acknowledgments

We would like to thank the following people for their contribution to
Educating the Heart and Mind: A History of Marymount School 1926-2001:

Sisters Kathleen Fagan, Jacquelyn Porter, Colette McManus, Maureen Vellon and Mary Alice Young, RSHM, Pat Barter, Cathy Callender, '60, Melissa Canoni, Maureen Flynn '64, Lynn Harvey, and Susan Johnson for their careful reading of the text and editorial contributions;

The members of the 75th Anniversary History and Archives Committees who worked tirelessly to provide the documents and photographic materials that make this volume such a rich representation of Marymount's history;

Susana Acosta and Dorothy Surella who have searched their files and given so generously of their time and memories to add depth and accuracy to the history;

Elvira M. Carota, MD, who, through her generous support of the Marymount Archives Project paved the way for this history;

Sisters Raymunde McKay, Mary Catherine Berchmans Walsh, and Majella Berg, RSHM for sharing their memories and to all others who were interviewed for this history;

Those who contributed their personal perspective to the history: Monika Anderson (sports), Pat Barter (capital campaigns), Kathy Birkey and Don Buckley (technology), John Crosson (boys at Marymount), Christopher Gray (the buildings), Kate O'Shea Donohue '63 (Sister Antoine Campbell), Annette Hayde and Christine Danielewski (the Parents' Association), Justine Hopper (a student's perspective), Lillian Issa (the Middle School), Robert Mulgrew and Matt Young (basketball), Venetia Oliver (sports, diversity, summer program), Kathryn Toohig '64 (Sister Raymunde McKay), and Beth Nielsen Werwaiss '61 (the Alumnae Association);

And, especially, Kathleen Birkey for her long hours of research and for organizing the history in a way that made it possible to draft this work, Lynn Harvey for her work and creative leadership with the photographic and memorabilia archives, Kathleen Harshberger, the outstanding Editor-in-Chief, who coordinated the project and finally, Beth NielsenWerwaiss '61, Chair of the 75th Anniversary Committee, for her leadership, inspiration and determination that this publication would become a reality.

Photo Credits: Diane Baasch, Leif Carlsson, Paul D'Innocenzo, Henry Krupka, Christina Krupka, '64, and George Sisting

Many of the photographs used in this history are held in the Marymount Archives or were taken from yearbooks, student newspapers or other school publications that did not identify the photographers. We are grateful to all of those photographers for leaving these valuable records.

Every effort has been made to present a true, accurate and comprehensive history of Marymount School. We apologize for any inaccuracies or oversights, and hope the reader will advise of such errors/omissions so that future editions of the history will have improved information on which to rely.

Design & Production:
Paul D'Innocenzo and Arne Lewis